THE GALLICAN
SAINT'S LIFE
AND THE
LATE ROMAN
DRAMATIC
TRADITION

Calliopius reading his recension of the Comedies of Terence to a Roman audience. MS Turonensis latinus 924, folio 13v. By courtesy of the Bibliothèque Municipale de Tours, France, and the Institut de Recherche et d'Histoire des Textes, Orléans.

THE GALLICAN
SAINT'S LIFE
AND THE
LATE ROMAN
DRAMATIC
TRADITION

E. CATHERINE DUNN

THE CATHOLIC UNIVERSITY OF
AMERICA PRESS

WASHINGTON, D.C.

Copyright © 1989
The Catholic University of America Press
All rights reserved
Printed in the United States of America

Library of Congress Cataloging-in-Publication Data
Dunn, E. Catherine (Ellen Catherine), 1916–
    The Gallican saint's life and the late Roman dramatic tradition /
by E. Catherine Dunn.
        p.   cm.
    Bibliography: p.
    Includes index.
    1. Christian drama, Latin (Medieval and modern)—Spain—History and
criticism.   2. Christian saints in literature.   3. Liturgical drama—History
and criticism.   4. Latin drama, Medieval and modern—Roman influences.
5. Latin drama—History and criticism.   6. Christian hagiography.
7. Catholic Church—Gallican rite—Liturgy—History.   I. Title.
PA8077.D86   1989
872'.03'09946—dc19   88-25784
ISBN 0-8132-0662-6

CONTENTS

PREFACE   vii
ABBREVIATIONS   ix

INTRODUCTION   1

I. JEAN MABILLON'S ESSAY ON THE
   GALLICAN LITURGY   17

II. THE MODERN QUEST FOR GALLICAN
    AND HISPANIC LITURGICAL TEXTS   35

III. THE TRADITION OF ROMAN DRAMA
     AND THE SAINT'S LIFE   46

IV. THE RECITATION OF THE SAINT'S LIFE IN
    THE GALLICAN AND HISPANIC LITURGIES   73

V. LITURGICAL DANCE AS SACRED DRAMA:
   THE HISPANIC PARADIGM   102

VI. JUGLARÍA AND THE DRAMATIC
    SAINTS' LIVES   122

CONCLUSION   140

SELECT BIBLIOGRAPHY   149
INDEX   161

PREFACE

The present study began with a search for the origins of the French and English saints' plays of the late Middle Ages, beyond the few Latin dramas of the twelfth century that survive today. In a number of exploratory essays centered on the so-called "farced epistles," I hoped to find a discernible growth of hagiographical drama from these medieval lections structured for two voices. They contained biographical material inserted or integrated into Scriptural passages concerned with holiness or a holy person. Although that hypothesis has still a historical validity, it has yielded in my thinking to a different theory that has led into earlier forms of dramatic saints' lives in the Gallican liturgy. The quest became more complicated as the Gallican texts, extant in only a few surviving missals and lectionaries, revealed affinities with sanctoral lections of the Hispanic liturgy roughly contemporary with those in Gaul (sixth and seventh centuries), and with those forms of chanted dramatic homilies occurring in the Byzantine liturgy of the same centuries.

Although I have listed in the final bibliography the pertinent essays written during this time of my exploration, and have sometimes drawn an idea or an allusion from them, I have excluded them from reprinting in this book, with one exception. That is the public lecture delivered at the Folger Library in 1981, and published as an article in 1984: "The Saint's Legend as *Mimesis*: Gallican Liturgy and Mediterranean Culture," reprinted from *Medieval and Renaissance Drama in England*, I, by permission of AMS Press, Inc.

A number of chapters here included were originally papers read at conferences held at the Medieval Institute, Western Michigan University. There the ideas I was suggesting were submitted to the discussion and questioning that make the sessions at Kalamazoo so stimulating. I owe a debt of gratitude to those who attended the sessions and encouraged me in the quest I had undertaken. I am also indebted to my own university for the generous support of my frequent travels to these sessions and for a grant in support of the final manuscript preparation, with a matching grant from the English Department's "Foley Fund." In 1981 there was a seminar, jointly directed by Professor O. B. Hardison and myself, at the Folger Shakespeare Library, at which I presented some of my theory.

Individuals at The Catholic University of America who aided me with bibliographical and linguistic problems in areas beyond my own specialization in medieval drama are Dr. Margaret Bates, Department of Modern Languages, and Dr. Thomas Halton, Department of Greek and Latin. I have appreciated also the courtesy and assistance of many at Mullen Library on our campus, the Library of Congress, the Folger Library and Dumbarton Oaks Library here in Washington, as well as the Eisenhower Library at Johns Hopkins University and the Walters Art Gallery in Baltimore. A special word of appreciation is due to Dr. Natalia Teteriatrikov, Director of the Princeton Index of Christian Art in the copy housed at Dumbarton Oaks Library. Dr. Julian Plante and Dr. Jonathan Black at the Hill Monastic Manuscript Library in Collegeville, Minnesota, have supplied detailed information on their holdings as indicated in my notes. My thanks go also to my capable typist, Miss Doris Vanecek, to those who assisted in the proofreading, Mrs. Parveen Elias, Mr. Robert Sheley, and Mrs. Kathleen Burns, and to my editor, Ms. Peggy Leonard.

E. C. DUNN
Washington, D.C.

ABBREVIATIONS FOR
SERIES PUBLICATIONS

CCSL	*Corpus Christianorum, Series Latina*
CSEL	*Corpus Scriptorum Ecclesiasticorum Latinorum*
DACL	*Dictionnaire d'Archéologie Chrétienne et de Liturgie*
DLG	*De Liturgia Gallicana Libri Tres*
MEL	*Monumenta Ecclesiae Liturgica*
MGH	*Monumenta Germaniae Historica*
NCE	*New Catholic Encyclopedia*
PL	*Patrologiae Latinae Cursus Completus*
RED	*Rerum Ecclesiasticarum Documenta*

THE GALLICAN
SAINT'S LIFE
AND THE
LATE ROMAN
DRAMATIC
TRADITION

INTRODUCTION

The origins of the medieval drama remain a fascinating mystery in our day in spite of the Carolingian troping movement that is still widely accepted as the starting point of this theatrical form. I have been studying the origins with a theory related to the Gallican liturgy: that the public recitation of saints' lives in this early medieval liturgy of Gaul was a form of drama in the Roman classical tradition. The theory has implications not only for drama produced on French soil, but also for that of Spain and Italy. This view discerns the rise of medieval drama several centuries earlier than the "Quem quaeritis" Easter tropes of the late Carolingian era, and it follows a different, though related, line from Professor O. B. Hardison's study of the Roman Mass as dramatic and as involved with the Carolingian tropes.[1]

The saint's life flourished in the liturgies of France, Spain, and northern Italy during the period of the sixth to eighth centuries. This was an era of Visigothic invasion in the Western Mediterranean and a time of military and political turmoil that induced the gradual collapse of Roman civilization in the provinces. It should not be surprising, therefore, that a theory about the dramatic importance of saints' lives as a cultural force would be difficult to prove. Explicit and formal documentation is about as easy to find as architectural ruins in a buried city. Documents there are—decrees of church councils like Toledo III, sermons of bishops like Caesarius of Arles, chronicles like that of Greg-

---

1. *Christian Rite and Christian Drama in the Middle Ages* (Baltimore: The Johns Hopkins Press, 1965).

ory of Tours. Most important of all, there are the saints' lives themselves in manuscripts and in editions like those of the *Monumenta Germaniae Historica* series. The evidence for the saint's *vita* recited in a public gathering is clearly available; but evidence that it was the leading cultural expression of a semi-barbaric populace and that it was an art form in the tradition of Roman drama—this documentation is not abundantly available.

The view here taken must therefore be partly deductive, drawn from the general cultural patterns of Western Mediterranean life in the late Empire, and from the pastoral needs of a half Christianized people, some of them native Latin inhabitants of Gaul and Spain, some of them the children of Germanic invaders. Mediterranean society has a stability and a clarity that have endured from century to century and, indeed, are still maintained in the social and cultural life of the present as the phenomenon that Albert Camus called "Mediterranean thought" (*la pensée méditerranéenne*). Its substructure remains that of antiquity in spite of the Christian life that has been built upon it, and many of its values are natural ones that can be called classical on the level of intellectual life and simply Graeco-Roman at the level of popular *mores* and folk ways. In the centuries following the fall of Rome the complex populations of Gaul, Spain, and Italy continued to live upon the cultural capital of the late Empire, sustained by the institutions and the wisdom of another day. Prominent among the elements of this heritage was the traditional entertainment of the popular theater, the mime and pantomime of the ancient world.

The present work, then, is a *reinterpretation* of records and documents from late antiquity and the early Middle Ages, and a study of Gallican liturgical texts in a new light. It presents a methodology, offering an approach to the problem that may open up opportunities for further research by others. I find two major schools of thought in opposition to my view, that of Karl Young in the mid-twentieth-century and that of Deconstructionism in the seventies and eighties. Turning first to the work of Young[2] and his associates, we may say that the historiography of the medieval drama in the twentieth century has been dominated by his authority, at least in America. His achievement in editing Latin liturgical drama was certainly splendid. His textual studies, however, gave him a position of influence that operated negatively in other areas of historical and theoretical criticism beyond his own specialization. He formulated principles that excluded research on his own part and intimidated his students and protégés from investigating or framing further hypotheses.

One of these principles was the independence of the Christian religious drama from a tradition of ancient classical Roman theater, and also from Eastern dramatic ceremonies of the early Christian centuries. Young opened his Introduction with this observation: "The dramatic manifestations to be considered in these volumes were the independent creation and possession of the medieval Church in Western Europe. They are to be regarded . . . as a spontaneous new birth and growth within the confines of Christian worship."[3] Although he simply ignored this historical background after deciding that it was irrelevant to the drama of the medieval church, one member of his "school" examined the Roman relationship in detail. Grace Frank, professor at Bryn Mawr College, became the spokeswoman on this question, an appropriate role for her to undertake, for she shared this interest with her husband, Tenney Frank, professor at Johns Hopkins University, and she cited articles of his composition as a basis for some of her own work. Briefly stated, her position, which she put into definitive form as the introductory chapter of her 1954 book,[4] was that classical Roman theater exercised virtually no influence on the medieval

2. Karl Young, *The Drama of the Medieval Church*, 2 vols. (Oxford: Clarendon Press, 1933).
3. Young, I, 1.
4. Grace Frank, *The Medieval French Drama* (Oxford: Clarendon Press, 1954).

religious drama. She also insisted that the medieval world knew little of ancient theater and that it labored under a basic misconception of classical drama, regarding the plays of Plautus, Terence, and Seneca as recited rather than acted before a Roman audience. At the fall of Rome in the late fifth century the classical theater ceased to exist, and only a scattering of nondescript entertainers survived into the Middle Ages to perpetuate popular traditions alien to the mainstream of formal Latin drama.[5]

In this way Grace Frank supported Young's denial of a continuity. Although I discuss her view below in Chapter III, I would say here that the most vulnerable part of it was her hypothetical attribution of the "misconception" to some copyist of a Terentian manuscript, who saw "Calliopius rec." in the text and thought the abbreviation stood for "recitavit" instead of "recensuit," thus making the editor Calliopius into a public performer reading aloud the play's lines.[6] The "misconception," however, was so widespread that it could not have resulted simply from an individual error in copying a manuscript.[7] In my judgment the case doesn't rest on some casual mistake by a person working with a text, but rather draws its power from a broad cultural context in the Mediterranean world from which a mode of theater developed and survived for centuries. This continuity of dramatic art is one of mimetic technique and of recitative, so pervasive in the Mediterranean world that it was often imported even into the literary plays of ancient comic and tragic writers, and was later borrowed by Christian liturgists throughout the Middle Ages. In this way the medieval era, instead of miscon-

5. Ibid., pp. 5, 17.
6. Ibid., p. 8.
7. Mary Marshall likewise made an elaborate case for medieval misconception of the *scena* in antiquity as a booth where poets recited. She suggested the origin of the misconception in a mistaken commentary of Remigius of Auxerre on a passage in Martianus Capella; this conception is widespread and unlikely to be a single commentator's error. (Marshall, "'Theatre' in the Middle Ages: Evidence from Dictionaries and Glosses," *Symposium*, 4 (1950), 1–39, esp. 17–18.)

ceiving the drama of late antiquity, knew it well as a theater of mime and recitation.

My own theory, as I have developed it in tracing the backgrounds of the Gallican saints' lives, rests upon the premise of this continuous mimic tradition. It is a matter of *techne*, a mode of expression that rests on a language of gesture, a *lingua franca*. It is capable of separation from any particular subject matter, and capable of realization in the domain of both the comic and the serious. It is vulnerable to moral censure when used in the comic mimes, but it is also capable of adaptation and refinement into the sublime art of tragic drama and of religious worship. Herein lies its dynamic, and its potential for a theater of recitative and pantomimic acting that lived far beyond the fall of Rome in the fifth century and lent itself to a Christianization centuries before the Carolingian Easter plays of the Benedictine monasteries.

In order to grasp this potential, one needs to understand that the nonverbal communication was a mode of expression in everyday ancient life itself, and then exercised a formative influence on the arts as well. The best study of this phenomenon is the book of Barthélemy Taladoire, *Commentaires sur la mimique*,[8] in which he recognizes a manual language that is apparently Sicilian Greek in origin but became a Mediterranean possession understood by all peoples of that extensive shore line. It is a set of conventional gestures that became symbols of meaning and that range from a simple hand message, like the rejection of a beggar's request for money, to a language of amorous intrigue. A sustained series of them tells a story and can be supported by a set of facial expressions, eye movements, the angle of the head, and so on.

Taladoire made his most important application of this mimic

8. A. Barthélemy Taladoire, *Commentaires sur la mimique et l'expression corporelle du comédien romain* (Montpellier: Déhan, 1951), pp. 102–06.

language to the ancient art of oratory as taught by Cicero and Quintilian. Both of them recognized that the orator's professional skill drew heavily upon the art of the mimic actor. They regarded delivery (which they called *actio*) as the most important part of rhetoric for the public speaker and they regarded this *actio* as a composite of disciplined breathing, posture, movement, and speech, all related to theatrical training and all cohering into a magnificent pattern or harmony that Cicero compared to the chords of a musical lyre.[9] Oratory is thus a conjunction of several arts that in their totality constitute an expression of soul through physical activity. The art of the tragic pantomimic actor came closer to this disciplined beauty than did the technique of the comic repertory, and Cicero as well as Quintilian warned the aspiring lawyer to be restrained by a sense of decorum in using the skills of the actor.[10] The very association in the Mediterranean experience of the mimic art with that of forensic oratory elevates, in my judgment, the level of the achievement represented by theatrical tradition and helps to explain why some of the same skills could become integral to religious worship and liturgical dance.

The Sicilian mimic technique, then, was a fertile source of artistic expression. No recognition of it appears in Young's or Frank's work. Their denial of a continuity in the Roman theatrical tradition into the Middle Ages became the view of literary history a generation ago, and prevailed in scholarly circles of the day. There is a partial similarity between Grace Frank's outlook and that of a more recent group known as the Konstanz School in southern Germany. The term "Rezeptionsästhetik" has become its designation, under the leadership of Hans Robert Jauss.[11] In America, one of its chief representatives is Clifford

9. Ibid., pp. 97–113. He cites the lyre analogy from Cicero, *De Oratore*, III, lvii, 216.

10. Ibid., pp. 107–21 et passim; Cicero, *De Oratore*, III; Quintilian, *Institutio Oratoria*, XI.

11. Jauss, "Theory of Genres and Medieval Literature," *Toward an Aesthetic of Reception*, tr. Timothy Bahti (Minneapolis: University of Minnesota Press, 1982),

Flanigan, who not only agrees with the denial of continuity between ancient and medieval drama, but has also expressed conviction that no liturgical practice of the Middle Ages transcended ritual or cult to become genuine drama before the twelfth century.[12] *The Fleury Play Book* contains the first plays, Dr. Flanigan contends, an outlook much more restrictive than his earlier one in which he found no medieval drama until after the Gallican rite had been suppressed in favor of the Roman in the eighth century.[13] "Rezeptionsästhetik," with its determination of genre and form by audience response to them, is a special form of Deconstructionism in current theory and of Phenomenology in the religious experience. This view is extra-literary in my judgment but comes to the same final conclusion on the relationship of medieval to Roman drama that the Young–Frank School had earlier championed.

In opposing the literary history represented by both of these schools, my hypothesis is that the Roman popular dramatic tradition was imitated in the sacred recitations of saints' lives in the Gallican period. There had been experiments in the Church with public devotion to the saints, as early as Augustine in North Africa and Prudentius in the Spanish liturgy. These tentative trials at a popular sanctoral devotion were sometimes narrative, sometimes lyrical, but from them grew a widely practiced custom of reading the saints' lives in public gatherings.[14] Peter Brown, referring to this practice in sixth-century Gaul, has called the reading a *psychodrame*, but he uses the term casually, and makes no literary attempt to implement his designation as

---

especially pp. 82–104; Rainer Warning, "On the Alterity of Medieval Religious Drama," *New Literary History*, 10 (1979), 265–92.

12. Flanigan, "The Fleury *Playbook* and the Tradition of Medieval Latin Drama," *Comparative Drama*, 18 (1984–85), especially pp. 362–72.

13. Flanigan, "The Roman Rite and the Origins of the Liturgical Drama," *University of Toronto Quarterly*, 43 (1974), 274.

14. B. de Gaiffier, "La Lecture des Actes des martyrs dans la prière liturgique en occident," *Analecta Bollandiana*, 72 (1954), 143. Justo Fernández Alonso attaches great importance to the hymns of Prudentius in the development of martyrs' lives in collections.

a theory of drama.[15] The tradition is a Spanish one, as far as the West is concerned, according to P. Salmon.[16] The Spanish custom is certainly one origin of the practice, and also contributed, in my judgment, a major component to the dramatic form of the experiments, namely, a stylized religious dance that is endemic to Hispanic life from its early history and closely related to the Roman phase of Spanish culture. This complex was destined to permeate the devotional life of the Western Mediterranean countries in various ways and various degrees, chiefly through the saints' lives read to congregations.

Young dismissed not only the Roman theater as an influence on medieval drama, as I have indicated, but also any impact of Byzantine dramatic form in the liturgy. He knew the work of George La Piana and of Vénétia Cottas on the dramatic homilies, especially the evidence for the procession of prophets in the Eastern liturgy as the prototype of the Latin prophet plays in Western Europe. He never confronted this scholarly view with a rebuttal, but simply condemned it with faint praise and went on with his work. The challenge to Young here has been the task of musicologists rather than of drama critics and it offers an intensely illuminating dimension to the historical problem.

Critical scholarship on the Byzantine liturgy shows a strange blend of conservatism and liberalism in the estimate of this liturgy's dramatic content and its influence on the religious drama of the West. From early studies like George La Piana's to recent ones like Egon Wellesz's there is a cautious recording of every phase of dramatic form, and an almost painful delineation of an evolutionary process from hymnic structure to dialogue, to dramatic homily, and at last to representational drama. Counterbalancing this scrupulous care to observe a gradual devel-

15. Brown, *The Cult of the Saints* (Chicago: University of Chicago Press, 1981), p. 82.

16. Pierre Salmon, ed., *Le Lectionnaire de Luxeuil, Collectanea Biblica Latina,* VII (1944), lxxvi, lxxxviii.

opment of drama up to the sixth century, there is a parallel statement, in quite absolute terms, that these Byzantine tendencies are the essential foundation of the liturgical drama of the West. Byzantinists seem to be saying at once too much and too little, and it is small wonder that Young dismissed them all with a sweeping denial. His rejection of Eastern dramatic origins, still a powerful negative force even in our generation, was ultimately based on a refusal to accept any semi-theatrical ceremonies, Eastern or Western, as genuine drama, without the explicit indication of costume, gesture, and full histrionic impersonation in the surviving texts themselves. His insistence upon the independent and spontaneous growth of Carolingian drama, like Frank's denial of Roman secular theater as background, sealed off an avenue of fruitful study for many years.

A review of the case for a Byzantine liturgical drama is nevertheless imperative for an understanding of the Gallican dramatic customs, because the Western practices of the sixth to eighth centuries are in some way indebted to a long and widely known tradition in the churches of the East. This relationship is crucial for the theory of origins as I am presenting it. In the last analysis, it may well be said that a Mediterranean tradition of mimetic form underlies both Byzantine drama and the contemporary Gallic experiments in the West. What I am suggesting is a comprehensive view of Eastern and Western techniques as a Mediterranean dramatic art known and available to those responsible for the Western liturgies.

Historians make it clear that the Byzantine era of greatest literary splendor occurred in the sixth and seventh centuries. The filiation of the Eastern poetic forms is a complex one, however, and some knowledge of the background behind the age of florescence is necessary if one is to isolate the distinctly Byzantine contributions and their possible influence on the Western European drama. The ultimate fount of Byzantine liturgical form is Hebraic poetry, a tradition of public Scriptural reading in which the Biblical lection is followed by a poetic homily. From

this source Syriac literature drew inspiration for a religious poetry best known in the hymns of St. Ephraim; but in this genre
the crowning achievement was that of Romanos, the mid-sixth-
century melodist of Byzantium, primarily in the literary and
musical type known as the *kontakion,* or dramatic homily.[17]

This term denotes a type of sermon, especially a Christmas
homily, sung as a descant on a liturgical text, using dialogue and
at times accompanied by mimic gesture of a stylized kind.[18] Romanos himself did not use the term *kontakion* for his compositions, but rather drew on a variety of words that indicated the
relationships of his work to poetry and music. The affinity of
the *kontakion* with lyrical expression is attested by the close relationship of the dramatic homily with the *troparion* and the *ka-
non,* both forms of religious lyric poetry, but the *kontakion* often
contained in addition a narrative line or a dramatic confrontation. All three of these genres are compositions for the Divine
Office rather than for the Mass, an important point for the potential development of drama here free of its involvement with
the sacred context of the Sacrifice itself.[19]

The struggle over the use of drama in the liturgy was especially severe in the East as a part of the Church's conflict with
the Arian heresy. The slow process of taking over the techniques
of the secular theater in the East developed from the recognition
by ecclesiastical authorities that the love of public spectacle, acting, and music could not be eradicated from the Christian populace, either by persuasion or by condemnation. This is a familiar story in ecclesiastical history and an element of the greatest

17. Egon Wellesz, *A History of Byzantine Music and Hymnography,* 2d ed. (Oxford: Clarendon Press, 1961), pp. 10–11, 359; Marjorie Carpenter, tr. *Kontakia of
Romanos, Byzantine Melodist* (Columbia: University of Missouri Press, 1970), pp.
xiii–xv.

18. Wellesz, p. 359; Carpenter, p. xv; George La Piana, *Le Rappresentazioni
sacre nella letteratura bizantina* (Grottaferrata: Tip. italo-orientale, S. Nilo, 1912), p.
58; J. Grosdidier de Matons, *Romanos le Mélode et les origines de la poésie religieuse
à Byzance* (Paris: Beauchesne, 1977), p. 3. Carpenter is the most cautious in admitting gesture or action.

19. Grosdidier de Matons, p. 3; Carpenter, p. xvi.

significance for the evolution of Christian culture in the Mediterranean world. One of the first to recognize this fact and to comprehend the value of histrionic resources for the pedagogical tasks of instructing the laity was the heretic Arius in the late third century. He is credited specifically with using the profession of the mimic actor in the diffusion of his tenets.[20] He is responsible also for the provocation of a reaction on the part of ecclesiastical leaders, impelling them to purge the heretical texts of their objectionable language but to retain the techniques of mimicry that had proven themselves effective with a populace in whom theater attendance was a way of life.

The mime as secular performance had centuries of history behind it. As indicated above, its origin was Sicilian Greek and its first artistic achievements were attributed to Sophron of Syracuse in Magna Graecia of the fifth century B.C. It became gradually a flourishing art in Rome, its dominance of the theater occurring there during the centuries of the Empire. It was this Roman mime, brought to a high degree of artistic perfection, that travelled back to the East and was reabsorbed there into the life of Christian Byzantium. The mimic actor became the most popular Byzantine performer and his type of skill displaced the tradition of ancient Greek drama (literary tragedy and comedy). In the East and in the West the trend and the outcome were identical: replacement of legitimate theater by the mimic mode.[21]

The transformation of ancient Greek drama into a mimic form is the most important element in Byzantine theatrical history. It was tragedy rather than comedy that served as basis here, because it offered the dignity and sobriety that could support a liturgical dramatic form in a Christian context. Egon Wellesz leads his colleagues in viewing this process as the importation of the Roman pantomime into Byzantine culture, making pos-

---

20. Vénétia Cottas, *Le Théâtre à Byzance* (Paris: Geuthner, 1931), pp. 60–62; Jack Lindsay, *Byzantium into Europe* (London: Bodley Head, 1952), p. 314.
21. Cottas, pp. 35–36; Wellesz, p. 88.

sible a nonrepresentational form of drama that consisted in recitative, ecclesiastical chant, and stylized gesture. The actor was
now known as a *tragados;* he was professionally a dancer, performing a thoroughly restructured set of histrionic roles derived
from ancient Greek tragedy, and gradually accepted as essentially symbolic in action rather than as recreation of real life on
the stage.[22]

Marius Sepet, a French archivist and historian of the late
nineteenth century, who was haunted all his life by a conviction
that Western medieval drama was indebted to ancient tragedy, missed the point made here by Wellesz, namely, that it
was a transformed ancient art that flourished in Byzantium and
passed on the dramatic tradition to the West. It was not the
work of Aeschylus, Sophocles, and Euripides. Sepet's own literary and dramatic instincts led him to his hypothesis, but also
kept him during his long scholarly career from actualizing his
intuitions in the absence of documentary evidence.[23] On just
this point there is now need for reassessment of the Mediterranean mimetic mode in the liturgy and ultimately in Western experiments related to liturgical drama.

Students of the Byzantine liturgy, in short, make a categorical
case for it as a recitative with musical and sometimes mimic
techniques from the fifth century onwards. While one or the

22. Wellesz, p. 88; Cottas, p. 48. Certain traditions about the composition of
whole representational plays as Christian exercises in transforming Greek pagan
drama have had currency from time to time, but present-day scholarship regards
these traditions with some skepticism. William Hone, for example, an antiquarian rather than a scholar, wrote about the work of Gregory Nazianzen surviving
in a Passion Play, the *Christos Paschon,* on the model of Greek tragedy. (*Ancient
Mysteries Described* [London, 1823, rpt. Singing Tree Press, 1969], p. 151.) This
play has been discussed by Sandro Sticca, in *The Latin Passion Play: Its Origins
and Development* (Albany: State University of New York Press, 1970) and in "The
Christos Paschon and the Byzantine Theater," *Comparative Drama,* 8 (1974), 13–44.
After reviewing the theories on Byzantine drama, pp. 16–18, Sticca continues
strongly in the article for Gregory's authorship of the *Christos,* pp. 26–41.

23. Sepet, *Origines catholiques du théâtre moderne* (Paris: Lethielleux, 1904), Preface. Allusions to Greek plays are scattered through his entire corpus of writings.

other hesitates to designate this liturgical complex as drama (e.g., Sandro Sticca[24]), even the conservative ones regard the technique as the origin of all liturgical drama, Eastern and Western. Carpenter, translating a passage from her mentor, George La Piana, says ". . . dramatic homily and sacred song gradually formed the sacred poetry of Byzantine literature, the *prototype of all subsequent sacred representational Christian literature.*"[25] Wellesz is no less absolute when he writes, in relation to dialogued Christian hymns of the fifth century: "We may regard the established cycle of the Nativity hymns, which obviously grew out of a smaller group in the early days of the Byzantine Church, as the prototype of the religious drama of the Middle Ages."[26] Statements of this kind might be dismissed as declarations of special interest, but the work of the Byzantinists is committed on a large scale to these general propositions and cannot be taken lightly.

Finally, apart from these Eastern scholars, several other well-known writers have entertained the possibility of a pagan tradition of mime influencing the Christian religious drama of the West. They have written in terms that I have found unacceptable in varying degrees, and I want to separate my own theory from theirs. As my allusions show in the chapters below, several approaches to a continuous mimic activity appear in the British work of E. K. Chambers,[27] in the German study of Hermann Reich,[28] as well as in the French monograph of Edmond Faral.[29]

24. Sticca expresses skepticism about the classification of Byzantine homilies or liturgical dialogues as drama, but regards the scholarly problem as still open ("The *Christos Paschon*," p. 21).

25. Carpenter, p. xxi, n. 34. The italics are in her text; the passage in La Piana's book is on p. 58.

26. Wellesz, p. 359.

27. Chambers, *The Mediaeval Stage*, 2 vols. (Oxford: Oxford University Press, 1903).

28. Reich, *Der Mimus* (Berlin: Weidmann, 1903; New York: G. Olms, 1974).

29. Faral, *Les Jongleurs en France au Moyen Âge* (Paris: Honoré Champion, 1910).

None of these writers, however, produce evidence for the period of the sixth to ninth centuries in the West, the great lacuna in the history of drama, the one I am attempting to fill.

Two works well-known in America, however, propose an especially challenging view, associating the professional secular mimic performers with trope writing itself in the French monasteries. These are the monographs of Benjamin Hunningher[30] and Oscar Cargill.[31] Both of them argue for the activity of secular mimes in the dramatic tropes, those musical and verbal insertions into the Carolingian liturgy. Hunningher, using iconographic evidence from a St. Gall psalter and a trope collection from St. Martial at Limoges, interprets the miniatures of dancing minstrels in the margins as evidence that the mimes themselves performed the tropes as drama.[32] Cargill, on the other hand, argues that the clergy became lax in liturgical prayer during the twelfth century and assigned the composition and performance of the tropes to secular minstrels (pp. 79–80). Both of these books have been seriously challenged on their historical accuracy by reviewers, and I will not repeat in detail the case against their conclusions.[33] My own theory offers a way of discerning mimic influence in a much earlier period, the Gallican, prior to the Carolingian era, and therefore independent of the troping movement itself.

A special observation should be made about Rosemary Woolf's reflection on the knowledge of ancient Roman drama possessed by twelfth-century writers. Although she was not concerned with early medieval drama, the second chapter of her

30. Hunningher, *The Origin of the Theater, An Essay* (The Hague: Nijhoff, 1955).

31. Oscar Cargill, *Drama and Liturgy* (New York: Columbia University Press, 1930).

32. Hunningher, pp. 68, 82, 127 n. 30.

33. For Karl Young's severe estimate of Cargill's book, see *The Drama of the Medieval Church*, I, 542–43, with reviews cited there; for a challenge to Hunningher's use of iconography, see Helena M. Gamer, "Mimes, Musicians, and the Origin of the Medieval Religious Play," *Deutsche Beiträge zur Geistigen Überlieferung*, 5 (1965), 9–28, and Sticca, *Latin Passion Play*, pp. 7–11.

English Mystery Plays[34] weighs the evidence for both a learned, scholarly awareness of ancient formal theater and a popular, grass-roots continuity of the mimic tradition in the High Middle Ages. Her chapter presents what she calls "a ragbag of scraps of evidence" for a secular current of drama parallel with the Latin religious plays of this century. Her ragbag is quite impressive, however, and even in her very cautious deductions she makes a good case for continuity, or at least recovery, of the ancient practices. Considering the allusions to Roman acting made by men like John of Salisbury and William Fitzstephen; the accessibility of Terentian and Plautine texts; the terminology for religious, liturgical plays that shows casual knowledge of Latin comedy; and even the existence of short texts known as *comoediae* and clearly imitated from Roman models—Woolf makes a stronger argument than a predecessor like Grace Frank had been willing to concede for a genuine renaissance of the twelfth century in this aspect of Western European culture. A carefully reasoned documentation of this kind makes a case for both a learned and a popular re-creation of the classical theater in the High Middle Ages (c. 1175–1250). I think it should also support the likelihood of such continuity in a historical period much closer to the era of the classics, an era still possessing a professional class of *mimi* that had survived the fall of Rome. This living heritage was still available in the sixth century, I believe, for a disciplined and devout use of the secular techniques in a Christian context.

To sum up, the danger in accepting the inclusive and far-reaching propositions about Byzantine or Roman origins is the difficulty of documenting a continuous tradition of dramatic development, especially in the East itself. Drawing conclusions seems to require a gigantic task of proof in details of influence. Karl Young refused to be convinced by any of it, but I think he

34. (Berkeley and Los Angeles: University of California Press, 1972), pp. 25–38.

was wrong. My own position is that the large view must be taken, and that the general history is one endemic to Mediterranean culture as a whole, rather than to narrow local lines of influence. The secular mime pervaded the whole Mediterranean world for centuries, and was known both in the East and in the West as a way of festive dramatic expression. It was capable of assimilation and adaptation by Christian liturgists, although it sometimes provoked a severely moral response and a strong condemnation by such thinkers as John Chrysostom and Augustine of Hippo. Against such a backdrop, the Gallican recitation of saints' lives takes on a broadly Mediterranean dimension and a dramatic cast, familiar for centuries in that area. We should now ask what the Gallican liturgy was and what were its cognate forms.

CHAPTER I

JEAN MABILLON'S ESSAY ON THE GALLICAN LITURGY

The work of the Benedictine scholars of St. Maur in the seventeenth century is one of the glories of France's *grand siècle*, and the leading representative of this learned confraternity is Jean Mabillon. The Maurists were a confederation of French Benedictine houses organized in 1618 for a special vocation of an intellectual character, comparable to that of the contemporary Belgian Jesuits known as the Bollandists, whose activity was more sharply defined in an editorial project—the *Acta Sanctorum*.[1] In small coteries of this type, French-speaking scholars have more frequently made their distinctive contributions to the intellectual life of Europe than in the formal academic faculties of a university campus. These groups demonstrate the principle that universities, by their very nature, tend to be conservative of the past and transmitters of the cultural heritage, while the original and creative projects of the mind are the work of small, extramural academies and societies that are free to explore and develop ideas.[2] The Bollandist coterie laid the foundations of modern scientific historiography, while the Maurists, under the leadership of Mabillon, created the science of diplomatics and formalized the history of ancient liturgical practices in Western Christendom.

1. David Knowles, *Great Historical Enterprises* (London: Thomas Nelson, 1963), pp. 37–38. Of the four essays in this book, one is devoted to "The Maurists" and one to "The Bollandists."

2. See Paul Kristeller, "Humanism and Scholasticism in the Italian Renaissance," *Byzantion*, 17 (1944–45), 353, for a different view.

Mabillon's greatest liturgical discovery was that of an old manuscript, the Luxeuil lectionary, a set of readings for the Mass and Divine Office. It revealed to him the complex world of the Gallican liturgy, which had flourished from the sixth to the eighth century; and he thus opened the way for his monograph of 1685 entitled *De Liturgia Gallicana Libri Tres*.[3] This masterful work remains to the present day an authoritative study that has weathered three hundred years of modern scholarship without being fundamentally superseded.[4] Although limited portions of the territory have been investigated (e.g., by Marignan and more recently by Salmon, and by Griffe),[5] no definitive modern study of the Gallican liturgy exists,[6] and the best method of exploring any phase of it today still requires Mabillon's book as its point of departure. Consequently, I have gathered the features of the Gallican liturgy that he regarded as distinctive, and will try to show their relationship to medieval liturgical drama, specifically to dramatic saints' lives.

Mabillon devoted most of *De Liturgia Gallicana* to the celebration of Mass and wrote a separate essay on the method of chanting the canonical Hours in the Divine Office (*De Cursu Gallicano Disquisitio*). When the two treatises are compared they reveal the same absorption in formal readings for Mass and Office, especially in the celebration of saints' days. Mabillon does not express philosophical reflection on the spirit or the style of the Gallican lectionary practices; he is the historian rather than the philosopher or literary critic, and his observations need to be

3. (Paris, 1685). I have used the text in the *Patrologiae Latinae Cursus Completus*, ed. J. P. Migne, hereafter referred to as *PL* (Paris: Garnier Fratres, 1878), Vol. 72. I have also seen the 1685 edition.

4. Henri Leclercq, *Mabillon* (Paris: Letouzey and Ané, 1953), I, 288–91.

5. A. Marignan, *Le Culte des saints sous les Mérovingiens* (Paris: Émile Bouillon, 1899). (This is Vol. 2 of his *Études sur la civilisation française*.) P. Salmon, *Le Lectionnaire de Luxeuil, Édition et étude comparative* (*Collectanea Biblica Latina*, 7 (1944) and 9 (1953); É. Griffe, *La Gaule chrétienne a l'époque romain*. 3 vols. (Paris: Picard, 1964).

6. Joannes Quasten, "Gallican Rites," *New Catholic Encyclopedia* (New York: Harcourt Brace, 1967), VI, 258, hereafter referred to as *NCE.*; G. Coless, "Recent Liturgical Study," *American Benedictine Review*, 22 (1971), 395.

interpreted in a larger context. From time to time modern historians have probed the devotional texture of this liturgy, and their general perceptions may help us momentarily to create an ambience for the hagiographical emphasis that Mabillon himself had discerned in the surviving Gallican texts and that will be explored later in the present study.

François Fétis, a late-nineteenth-century French musicologist, was among the first modern writers to show interest in the Gallican liturgy. The feature that he found most striking was the dramatic style of its Mass celebrations and of its psalmody, litanies, and processions. Fétis attributed this dramatic quality to the Eastern affinities of the Gallican. While the Oriental origins or importations into the liturgical practices of Gaul remain even today a vexed and disputed question, nevertheless the dramatic texture of these ceremonies is of genuine importance in itself to the development of medieval theatrical form in the West.[7] Another early discussion of Gallican style was the essay of Edmund Bishop, first published in 1899, and considered a classic, if antiquarian, study of the creative, poetic, and dramatic flair of the Gallican in contrast with the reserve and austerity of the Roman manner.[8] Older studies like these two tend to be defensive of the freedom and creativity in the one rite in comparison with the classical gravity and sublimity of the other. A rather clear dichotomy of attitudes has been noticeable in our century for and against the superior sophistication of the Roman style, and the conflict of view has been especially notable among French liturgists.

Henri Leclercq, for example, has probed the cultural conditions accounting for the differences between the two.[9] He

7. Fétis, *Histoire générale de la musique* (Paris: Didot, 1876), V, 107.

8. Bishop, "The Genius of the Roman Rite," reprinted in *Liturgica Historica: Papers on the Liturgy and Religious Life of the Western Church* (Oxford: Clarendon Press, 1918).

9. Leclercq, "Gallicane (Liturgie)," *Dictionnaire d'archéologie chrétienne et de liturgie* (Paris: Librairie Letouzey and Ané, 1924), Vol. 6, Col. 480; hereafter referred to as *DACL*.

speaks of the Gallican Mass as characterized by visual beauty and spectacle, and an auditory splendor in its fine choral music. Both of these aesthetic elements served to encourage contemplation and prayer, and to invite participation of the faithful in a joyful response to the mystery of the sacrifice.[10] The Roman Mass, on the other hand, is expressive of a central authority conscious of its universal interests and heavy responsibilities. Its manner is grave, simple, and majestic—a bit severe—discouraging lyrical response, individual variation of the prayer formulas, and popular participation in the verbal texture. Here the celebrant becomes spokesman for the community rather than its choral leader, blocking much of the spontaneous expression, even the joyful shouting, that had characterized the Gallican congregational activity.

In our own generation prominent studies of the Roman liturgy have contributed to the sharpness of discordant views. The editorial work of Emmanuel Bourque[11] on the Roman sacramentaries and of M. Andrieu on the *Ordines Romani*[12] has contained disparaging estimates of the chaos and disorganization in Gallican liturgical customs and texts by comparison. The basic question is whether *creativity* is constructive genius or simple anarchy. The strongest defender of Gallican order and control has been Pierre Salmon, who has met the charges of Bourque and Andrieu by declaring that the Gallican texts reveal a solid, organized, and generally uniform base in essentials, but at the same time a degree of local variation in superficial matters under the approval of the diocesan ordinary or of synodal decrees.[13] Cyrille Vogel, moreover, has indicated that the liturgy of the papal city at the time of the Frankish importation of it was

10. Professor Hardison speaks of congregational participation in the Gallican Mass, even the shouting of joyful response. (*Christian Rite,* p. 53 n. 52.)

11. Bourque, *Étude sur les sacramentaires romains* (Roma: Instituto Pontificio di Archeologia Cristiana, 1949), I, 27.

12. Michel Andrieu, *Les 'Ordines Romani' du haut moyen âge,* 5 vols. (Louvain: "Spicilegium sacrum lovaniense" Bureaux, 1931–61), II, viii–xxi.

13. Salmon, *Le Lectionnaire,* IX, 50–51.

not marked by a superior beauty of style. The motive for the suppression of the Gallican was not aesthetic: "L'on n'avancera pas, j'imagine, une quelconque supériorité de la liturgie romaine sur le culte célébré '*more gallicano*,' surtout si l'on songe à ce qu' était la liturgie dans la ville papale entre les années 700 et 800, et ce qu'avait été et pouvait être encore le cérémonial grandiose dont témoignent Césaire d'Arles, Grégoire de Tours et le pseudo-Germain de Paris."[14]

Defenders of both rites find words like "grandiose" and "sublime" to be suitable adjectives for their respective liturgies but with different connotations. What needs to be remembered is that the Gallican style lived on surreptitiously, embedded in the Roman as practiced in the Frankish mode after 789, in which more than a little of the Gallican "grandiose" tinged the Roman classical "sublimity." But this is another story.[15]

Still a third quality may be added to those of popular participation and dramatic style in the description of Gallican custom. It is the spirit of relaxed gaiety and holiday play that attended the celebration of a saint's festival. O. M. Dalton, a commentator on Gregory of Tours' *Historia Francorum*, writes about an early tradition of festive gatherings for saints' days in pre-Merovingian Gaul, at which a special liturgical celebration would be followed by social entertainment among the laity who were in attendance, including games of dice and ball-playing as well as narrating of stories.[16] The accounts of such celebrations suggest a pilgrimage atmosphere surrounding the shrine of a saint rather than the ordinary devotional life of a country par-

14. Vogel, "Le Développement historique du culte chrétien en occident," *Problemi di storia della Chiesa: l'Alto Medioevo* (Milano: Vita e Pensiero, 1973), II, 93.

15. Burkhard Neunheuser, "Die Römische Liturgie in ihren Beziehungen zur Fränkisch-Germanischen Kultur und der Tropus," in *Dimensioni drammatiche della liturgia medioevale: Atti del I Convegno di Studio Viterbo* (Viterbo: Bulzoni Editore, 1977), 161–68. Clifford Flanigan has also written well of this Gallo-Roman period and its complex liturgy, in "The Roman Rite and the Origins of the Liturgical Drama," *University of Toronto Quarterly*, 43 (1974), 263–84.

16. *The History of the Franks*, by Gregory of Tours, trans. O. M. Dalton, 2 vols. (Oxford: Clarendon Press, 1927), I, 339.

ish, and the recitation of the beloved saint's life in the Mass of the day seems to have been the normative feature of the generally heightened and festive context surrounding the saint's day.

When the hagiographical interests of the Gallican texts are considered in the light of the external splendor, the dramatic style, and the joyful ethos of the prayer life, the texts constitute a matrix that may well be the background of the medieval liturgical drama. This theory bypasses the troping phenomenon of the Carolingian era in favor of an earlier dramatic context predating the Frankish imposition of the Roman rite in Gaul. It would be an error to attribute such a theory to Mabillon himself, but his careful study of the four salient features in Gallican missals provides a basis for this deduction.

Without entering deeply into the obscure development of this old liturgy and becoming entangled in its relationships to Eastern worship, Mabillon probed the Gallican place in the Latin rite and attempted to situate it historically. He distinguished four basic liturgies among peoples of the Latin rite: Roman, Ambrosian (Milanese), Hispanic (Mozarabic), and Gallican.[17] He did not make a place for a British category. He then centered his attention on the Hispanic and Gallican. He found these agreeing in fundamental ways that separated them from Roman usage, especially in the celebration of Mass. Although he did not use exact dates, he apparently extended the liturgy on French soil until 789,[18] the Council of Aix-la-Chapelle, which reimposed the Roman rite. It is not clear whether he regarded the first two or three centuries of the Christian era as ones of the Roman rite in Gaul, as Father Quasten does, and as H. Le-

---

17. *De Liturgia Gallicana*, Bk. I, Col. 114. Hereafter referred to as *DLG*.
18. *DLG*, Col. 127, 30, 7. Mabillon quotes Abbot Hilduin's phrase about the age of the Gallican customs: "'ab initio receptae fidei.'" See also col. 127, 30, 8. Father Richard Donovan, in *The Liturgical Drama in Medieval Spain* (Toronto: Pontifical Institute of Mediaeval Studies, 1958), pp. 20–21, speaks of the Mozarabic in a different way. Strictly, it is the liturgical practice of Christians in Spain during the centuries of Arab rule, but fundamentally it is the Spanish liturgy, with features dating even to Apostolic times, and is therefore very old. The term "Hispanic" is preferable to "Mozarabic," and I use it in the present study.

clercq denies. Mabillon used the term "liturgia Gallicana" as a singular one, not distinguishing an earlier, heterogeneous phase from a later unity, as modern scholars do,[19] and not adverting to the general conditions which militated against a closely knit and uniform set of observances. Salmon, for example, has pointed out that the Gallican era was one of recurrent political turmoil and religious persecutions marked by periods of decline in the level of ecclesiastical culture and in the linguistic equipment necessary for careful regulation of service books.[20]

Mabillon discussed four special features of Mass celebration that he took to be the distinguishing marks of the Gallican observance and of the closely related Hispanic one. It is the clustering of these features that the Gallican missals reveal with enough uniformity to separate them from contemporary Mass *ordines* and quite clearly from Roman practice. These four characteristics had already been suggested by his seventeenth-century predecessor, Cardinal Joannes Bona, whom he credited as the first one to know anything about Gallican observance after its disappearance in the late Carolingian era.[21] All four of the practices are concerned with public readings in the Mass, and this very fact serves to underscore the importance to the Gallican service of what we now call "the liturgy of the word," the recitations that precede the sacrificial action of the Mass. These lections suggest a tradition that may be related to the drama of late antiquity, and may be listed as: (1) the use of three

19. J. Quasten (*NCE*, VI, 258) writes of Gallican liturgies as existing in local forms until the sixth century, when a common set of features can be distinguished. He favored the early liturgy of Gaul (in the Patristic era) as the Roman rite, but H. Leclercq opposed this idea, favoring the Ambrosian rite as the early form used in Gaul. (*DACL*, Vol. 6, Col. 477.)

20. Salmon, VII, lxxvii–lxxviii.

21. *DLG*, Preface, cols. 103–4, and Bk. I, cols. 121–22. Cardinal Bona's work is *Rerum Liturgicarum Libri Duo* (Coloniae: Hermannus Demen, 1674). Chapter XII, especially pp. 121ff., deals with the Gallican Mass. The Cardinal made it clear that he did not have the leisure to work out the scholarly problems involved in his fragmentary texts (p. 123).

regular lections (prophetic, apostolic, and evangelical), to be explained; (2) the recitation of the passions of martyrs; (3) the nar-
ration of confessors' lives and miracles; (4) formal calls for silence in the congregation before the various readings.

The normal assignment of three lections to the Mass is of fundamental importance in Mabillon's account. This practice did
not originate in Gaul, but it was preserved there long after it
was discontinued in the Roman liturgy of the fifth century.[22]
The custom is Eastern in its ultimate source, as the ancient
liturgies of Syria, Byzantium, and Armenia indicate,[23] and may
date to Apostolic times.[24] The three readings are termed "prophetic," (i.e., from the Old Testament), apostolic (from the New
Testament Epistles), and evangelical (the Gospel selection).[25]

These three lections in sequence have early testimony in
Gaul. There is a sixth century pastoral letter written by Caesarius of Arles that contains clear reference to them. Mabillon, in
commenting on the letter, emphasizes Caesarius' admonition to
his people as showing that the prophetic lection from the Old
Testament was being used at this time. The bishop was urging
the congregation to attend the whole Mass and not to leave after
the three lections.[26] (A modern reader is likely to be more force-
fully struck by the irony that Caesarius reveals when he must
proclaim that the Mass is not over when the three lections have
been read.) The sacred ceremonies, he insisted, were incomplete until the consecration of the bread and wine into the Body
and Blood of Christ. Moreover, he observed, the people could
read or hear the prophetic, apostolic, and evangelical lections in

22. Louis Duchesne, *Origines du culte chrétien* (Paris: Ernest Thorin, 1889), p.
160; P. Salmon, VII, 13.

23. J. Quasten, "Oriental Influence in the Gallican Liturgy," *Traditio*, 1 (1943),
64–65.

24. Dom Edmond Martène, another of the Maurists, regarded the practice as
probably of Apostolic origin. See his *De Antiquis Ecclesiae Ritibus Libri Quattuor*
(Rotomagi: Guillelmus Behourt, 1700), I, 367 (Bk. I, Ch. iv, art. 4).

25. The practice was followed in the Hispanic liturgy of this period and was
retained there until modern times (Quasten, "Oriental Influence," pp. 64–65).

26. *DLG*, Col. 126, 27–28, 4.

their homes, but only in the house of God could they attend the Consecration.

The Gallican books themselves do not reveal a uniform practice in the matter of the three lections. P. Salmon has counted only thirty-eight Masses in the Luxeuil Lectionary containing the three, out of a total fifty-two. In the Bobbio Missal the count is fourteen out of fifty-eight. He considers this small ratio as typical of Gallican customs.[27] The ratio may simply be, however, an indication that the practice was confined to certain types of feast days, as it is now, when a revival of the three readings has become once more a feature of the Roman liturgy. The small ratio may also reflect the substitution of special saint's day readings for the Scriptural lessons.

The second and third characteristics of the Gallican Mass are closely related to the retention of three lections, and, indeed, are a special modification of this custom. One is the reading of a martyr's passion and death story on the day of his festival, and the other is the recitation of a "confessor's" life and miraculous powers on his day. Mabillon says that some sanctoral feasts, like that of St. Dionysius (Denis) have in their Masses brief references to the martyrdom, while in others the entire *acta* are read, as in the case of St. Aemilian.[28] He cites scattered references to the practice in Gregory of Tours' various works, for example, the reading of St. Polycarp's passion and that of St. Martin.[29] He calls attention to a letter of Charles the Bald, and to that of Abbot Hilduin to Louis the Pious.[30] In Charles' letter, he was referring to the basic affinity of the Gallican and Hispanic rites as he had discovered it, in the late Carolingian era, and Mabillon, in commenting, singled out the recitation of the saints' lives as illustrative of the affinity: "Certe Hispani vitas

27. *Le Lectionnaire de Luxeuil*, IX, 55.
28. *DLG*, Col. 122.
29. *DLG*, Col. 133.
30. Ibid., Cols. 121–22. Hilduin was Abbot of St. Denys; his addressee Ludovicus Augustus (Louis the Pious). See H. Netzer, *L'Introduction de la messe romaine en France sous les Carolingiens* (Farnborough: Gregg, 1968), p. 6.

sanctorum (quod de Gallis tradit Hilduinus) in sacris etiam publicis recitabant. . . .[31] There is important additional evidence in
the *Expositio Brevis,* a letter that Mabillon did not know of. It
was discovered by another Benedictine, Edmond Martène,
about 1700, and was incorrectly attributed by him to St. Germain de Paris. It is, however, a document of the Gallican era,
and speaks of the lections being varied according to the season
of the year, for example, the *Apocalypse* of St. John featured in
Paschal times, "vel gesta sanctorum confessorum ac martyrum
in solemnitatibus eorum. . . ."[32]

The reading of the saint's life was a substitution for one or
two of the other Mass lections (prophetic or apostolic). Mabillon
does not give detailed information on this point, but he speaks
clearly of the Mass itself as the context of the recitation. In the
sentence above, where he compares Gallican and Spanish practice (Col. 122), he cites the life of the abbot Aemilian written by
the Spanish bishop Braulio in order that it could be read as
much as was feasible in the Mass of the feast day: "quem libellum ideo conscripsit 'ut posset in missae ejus celebratione quantocius legi,' quemadmodum Braulio ipse in Praefatione sua loquitur."[33] Salmon throws more light on the practice, indicating
in his study of the Luxeuil service book that the first reading
(the prophetic) and even the second one (the apostolic) could
be replaced by the saint's life of the day; he adds a most important detail, that the recitation of the life would have been started
in the Matins office, and the part not completed in the night
office would be read in the Mass.[34] This is apparently what Mabillon meant in saying that Braulio's life of St. Aemilian was

31. *DLG,* Col. 122, 20–21.
32. *Expositio Brevis Antiquae Liturgiae Gallicanae in Duas Epistolas Digesta,* ed.
Migne, *PL,* Vol. 72, Cols. 90–91. Migne also prints Martène's commentary on
the letters, and I have preferred this edition because of its context. A version has
been edited more recently by Klaus Gamber as *Ordo Antiquus Gallicanus* (Regensburg: Friedrich Pustet, 1965), which I have used as well.
33. *DLG,* Col. 122. See below, for Braulio's work.
34. Salmon, IX, 56.

written to be read as much as was feasible (*quantocius*) in his Mass celebration.

The last of the Gallican features noted by Mabillon is the practice of imposing silence upon the congregation at various points in the Mass celebration. He had found reference to this custom in Gregory of Tours' *Historia* (Lib. 7, Ch. 8), but was puzzled by Gregory's failure to "place" these calls for attention. Mabillon sought supporting evidence of a more explicit kind in cognate liturgies, that is, in the Hispanic and Ambrosian, with some success. In general, the call for silence was another way of emphasizing the importance of public reading. It was an admonition for attentive listening to the word of God. As the pseudo-Germain put it, the deacon called for the people to be silent in order that they might better hear the word (in the physical process of listening in a large crowd) and also that they might the better assimilate the message into their hearts.[35]

Parallel customs in the other liturgies mentioned above convinced Mabillon that the Gallican imposition of silence occurred before both the Epistle and Gospel lections.[36] He found one discussion of it that is quite intriguing in the Ambrosian celebration of the Rogation Days. The appeal for attention occurred before a reading from the Gospel *preceding* the Mass: "'Diaconus dicit: Parcite fabulis. Custos item: Silentium habete. Et alter respondet: Habete silentium.'"[37] The phrase that leaps from the page is "parcite fabulis," put aside conversation (perhaps), and even stories or plays. It suggests that the people assembled for the ceremony might have been listening to recited saints' lives until the time of Mass itself. There are comparable references to silence and "fabulae" in sermons of Caesarius of Arles, who ruled that the laity attending the recitation of the Divine Office should be trained to chant psalms and hymns, in the manner of clerics, in order that they should not have leisure to be en-

35. *Expositio Brevis*, Col. 89.   36. *DLG*, Cols. 122–23.
37. Ibid., Col. 116.

grossed in "fabulae" in church. This word, already in Classical Latin, had the distinct meanings of "conversation," "story," and even "a play." I think, however, that the allusions here, though tempting, do refer to "conversation" rather than to stories or plays.[38] (See Chapter III, below, n. 22, for a consideration of the word in other contexts.)

There is scattered evidence that the admonition to careful listening occurred also before certain prayers in the Mass. The pseudo-saint Germain refers to a call for silence as the celebrant entered for Mass accompanied by the chanting of an antiphon.[39] H. Netzer refers to this placing of the appeal at the very start of the ceremony, and a parallel call for silence between the Mass of the Catechumens and the opening of the sacrifice proper at the Offertory.[40] All of the cryptic references to the custom point toward a great stress on the word and the importance of readiness to receive it with open hearts.

Mabillon's consideration of the Divine Office in the Gallican observance occurs in an essay appended to his major work and is entitled "De Cursu Gallicano Disquisitio." In the recitation of the canonical hours there is even less evidence of uniformity than in the celebration of Mass. Such a lack of regulation is understandable in view of the great antiquity in the texts and records, since the Gallican era dates back at least to the fifth century. Moreover, most of the evidence available is from secular, that is, diocesan sources rather than monastic ones, and local regulation by the bishop tended to diversity rather than unity of practice. What emerges from Mabillon's essay is a pic-

38. Mabillon, *De Cursu*, Cols. 395–96, 403 ("ut non haberent spatium in ecclesia fabulis occupari") (from Cyprian's *Vita* of Caesarius, actually a work written by Cyprian and several others). Caesarius, *Opera Omnia*, ed. G. Morin (Maretioli, 1942), II, 296. See Caesarius' Sermons 13, 55, 77, 78, and 80 for admonitions to silence in church; see also *Oxford Latin Dictionary* (Oxford: Clarendon Press, 1977) under the word, "fabula."

39. *Expositio Brevis*, Col. 89.

40. Netzer, pp. 3–4, 8.

ture of local autonomy, with a rather strong opposition between two leading centers of episcopal authority, Lyons and Arles, the first representing a tradition of Roman gravity and the second a fostering of the Gallican tendencies toward freedom and spontaneity in expression. It may well be that the survival of texts in one or another local area has contributed to a sense of dichotomy that was not really so sharp in the actual situation during the centuries involved. The city of Arles figured prominently in the liturgical life of Gaul because of its famous sixth-century bishop, Caesarius, and Lyons had a similar prominence three centuries later when Agobard emerged as a defender of the reestablished Roman rite and the censor of the Gallican practices that were still eliciting ardent support in the early ninth century.

Mabillon writes of the Matins office under two forms in the churches of Gaul, the one a ferial recitation on ordinary days, referred to as "Matutinae," and the other a solemn form on major feasts, designated as "Vigiliae." The more festive Matins was a preparation for the great day and was truly a night office, begun at least by midnight of the evening before.[41] It is in this form that the celebration of a saint's day is to be found as a splendid ceremony, attended by the laity, who would remain for the solemn Mass. Herein lies the importance of recitations in a festive manner, beginning the saint's *vita* in the Matins office and continuing it during the Mass lections.

Only certain churches would have choral recitation of the office in this manner, and practice varied throughout the territory and from one era to another. In some districts, for example, clergy of small parishes were appointed to regular times at which they were responsible to chant the office in a cathedral or basilica, so that a rotation system assured the complete and centralized recitation of the Hours throughout the week. Bishops urged their diocesan laity, even in rural areas, to attend Mass,

41. Mabillon, *De Cursu*, Col. 405, 421, 53.

Matins, and Vespers on Sundays and feast days, as did Riculfus, a ninth-century bishop of Soissons.[42] Caesarius of Arles had urged his flock on occasion to attend the Little Hours—the short prayer services at three-hour intervals through the day—observing that he was not asking too much of them, as the required time was only six hours![43]

The persuasive efforts of Caesarius were a powerful force not only in the town of Arles but in the neighboring territory of southeastern Gaul, including Marseilles. Mabillon records from the sermons of this zealous bishop, and from his biography, that Caesarius urged his people to hear the lections of the Divine Office read in church and also to read them, or hear them read, in their own homes.[44] Specifically, he mentioned the reading of *passiones*, which Mabillon clarifies as "passiones martyrum" read at "Vigiliis matutinis" (solemn Matins). Aurelian of Arles, a contemporary author of the *Regula ad Monachos*, also referred to the recitation of martyrs' passions on their feast days; indeed, he prescribed it, and justified the practice by a decree of the third Council of Carthage.[45]

Conciliar decrees form a confusing background to this liturgical history, since local councils vary and even contradict one another on the point. Mabillon cites the fourth Council of Toledo (canon 12), Agde (canon 30), and Tours (canon 23) as favorable to the use of devotional materials in hymns and lec-

42. Ibid., Col. 403, 417, 47. Fortunatus, a sixth century priest and poet, gives a glowing account of the Divine Office as celebrated at the cathedral church of St. Germain de Paris, in which not only the diocesan clergy took part but also the laity, accompanied by musical instruments. The account has often been quoted, from Mabillon to Pierre Riché. See Fortunatus, *Opera Poetica*, ed. Fridericus Leo, *MGH* (Berolini: Weidmann, 1881), IV, 37–39.

43. Salmon, IX, 64 n. 101.

44. Mabillon, *De Cursu*, Col. 396, 404–5. Citations are to Sermons 140, 288, and 300 throughout the description of Arles' customs.

45. Ibid., Col. 397, 407, 34. G. R. Coffman mentions Aurelian's reference to this custom and speaks of it as the origin of breviary lections. See his *New Theory Concerning the Origin of the Miracle Play* (Diss. Univ. of Wisconsin: Menasha, 1914), p. 35. Mabillon mentions that Ferreolus Ucetiensis (Uzès) urges the reading of martyrs' *passiones* in Chapter 18 of his Rule (*De Cursu*, Col. 398).

tions, even if taken from non-Scriptural sources.[46] On the other hand, he notes that the councils of Braga (canon 12) and Laodicea (canon 59) were hostile to freedom of this kind. The whole question involves much more than saints' lives, as H. F. Muller writes, and is concerned over the early centuries of the Church with problems of heresy from time to time, when both hymns and saint stories could be the vehicles of unauthorized doctrines in periods of controversy. Moreover, when such materials were written without supervision, they could be marked by ignorance and lack of sophistication, however well-intentioned.[47] In the Merovingian age, Muller says, the decline of Latin and the rise of primitive Romance dialects meant often the composition of badly written, even barbaric attempts at devotional material. He interprets the later imposition of the Roman liturgy by Charlemagne as essentially a movement to ensure competent Latin expression in an unlearned age.[48]

The explicit prohibition of saints' lives as lection material, however, was more than a concern over linguistic or cultural competence. It appears to have been a Roman attack against Gallican and Hispanic practice, indeed, against the most salient feature of those liturgies. The Roman viewpoint was perennially opposed to the reading of saints' lives in church because of the difficulty posed for ecclesiastical authority in assuring a manner befitting the sacred ceremonies. Martène, after observing that in the early Church, lections might be taken not only from the Bible but also from the letters of bishops and popes, noted that later "in concilio Laodiceno can. 59. & Carthaginensi III. can. 47. prohibitum fuit ne libri praeter canonicos novi ac veteris testamenti publice legerentur."[49] He went on to indicate "de gestis

---

46. *De Cursu*, Cols. 393–4, 400.
47. Muller, "Pre-History of the Mediaeval Drama: The Antecedents of the Tropes and the Conditions of their Appearance," *Zeitschrift für Romanische Philologie*, 44 (1924), 544–75.
48. Muller, p. 553.
49. Martène, *De Antiquis*, I, 367.

sanctorum Martyrum" that they were specifically excluded by this tradition: "Secundum antiquum consuetudinem singulari cautela in ecclesia Romana non leguntur," a statement he attributed to Pope Gelasius, but which was probably a sixth-century decree, and was frequently repeated.[50]

The imposition of the Roman liturgy upon Gaul in the Frankish kingdom was, therefore, a major confrontation on many points, but especially on the use of non-Scriptural lections. It struck at the very roots of Gallican festivity on saints' days.

Agobard of Lyons, at the end of the Gallican era, draws upon the armory of Roman prohibitions, conciliar and other, to discredit all manifestations of popular composition and unauthorized narratives in liturgical services. Although Agobard represents the Carolingian reform as it had advanced into the early ninth century, he throws much light upon Gallican customs for us simply by condemning them. He urges that there be a uniform Mass *ordo*, a uniform lectionary, and a standard antiphonary,[51] all of them admitting only authorized material. Essentially, Agobard seems concerned about restriction of Divine praises to the words of Scripture itself and he thunders against imaginative composition and human errors, even if poetically expressed. He cites conciliar prohibitions against these things, and perhaps best states his position in the reform of the antiphonary, insisting that it be "'humanis figmentis et mendaciis expurgatum'" (purified from human fictions and lies).[52]

I have made Mabillon's work the point of departure for the present study, because of his emphasis on the fundamental importance that saints' lives held in Gallican life. There has been an intense interest in recent years in the cult of the saints, es-

---

50. Ibid.; Muller, p. 549.
51. Mabillon, *De Cursu*, Col. 394, 401, 26.
52. Ibid., 400, 26. Agobard is quoted as referring to conciliar decrees: "'Sed et reverenda concilia patrum, inquit, decernunt, nequaquam plebeios psalmos in Ecclesia decantandos; et nihil poetice compositum in divinis laudibus usurpandum.'"

pecially of their relics, during the early centuries of Christianity. The studies have not been liturgical in content, but rather have placed the hagiographical devotions in the context of late Roman social and political institutions in the declining Empire. Peter Brown has been a major contributor to this scholarly endeavor, in *The Cult of the Saints: Its Rise and Function in Latin Christianity,*[53] and made the devotion to the saints in Gaul a particularly prominent example of the cult. He sees the phenomenon as an adaptation of ancient Roman concepts of patronage. The relationship of pagan Romans to their gods and to natural forces controlling their destinies was gradually transformed into a relationship of affection for saintly persons who after death gave patronage, especially miraculous healing, to their Christian devotees. Raymond Van Dam, on the other hand, presents rather harshly the cult of saints' relics as a form of superstitious devotion, through which people of Gaul found a replacement for the cult of the Roman Empire in their provincial consciousness, as they attempted to rebuild an imperial society on the rubble of the collapsing Roman authority.[54]

These studies offer a very different approach to Gallican sanctoral piety from Mabillon's, but they complement his liturgical materials with evidence from the political and social life in Gaul of the fourth, fifth, and sixth centuries. Mabillon did not think in these terms, but rather in religious categories; yet his works gain an advantage by juxtaposition with modern social studies that treat the hagiographical interests as the central fact of Gallican life. These modern investigations can gain in return a dimension from the materials of Mabillon, which reflect a Gallican culture more richly humanistic than it would otherwise seem to be. The great stress on the word of God in the Mass and the

53. Chapter III of Brown's book is especially valuable here.
54. Van Dam, *Leadership and Community in Late Antique Gaul* (Berkeley and Los Angeles: University of California Press, 1985), pp. 170–78, and Part IV: "The Cult of Relics in Sixth-Century Merovingian Gaul."

Office and its formal reading reveal a prayer life that transcends a mere cult of relics and forms part of a richer spirituality. The present chapter is confined to Gallican customs in Mabillon's own terms; subsequent chapters explore the relationships of these recitations to a long tradition of public reading, both secular and religious.

CHAPTER II

THE MODERN QUEST FOR GALLICAN
AND HISPANIC LITURGICAL TEXTS

The bibliographical problem of locating materials in Gallican service books is extraordinarily difficult because only a few examples of any liturgical type have survived from that period into modern times. When this liturgy was suppressed by the Frankish clergy and the royal authority, it seems to have disappeared quickly throughout most of Gaul, perhaps by organized destruction of the official texts themselves. Although a particular locale like the diocesan see of Langres might continue to use the old missals and lectionaries even into the twelfth century, as Dom Salmon has determined,[1] such conservatism was rare,[2] and even a theoretical knowledge of the liturgical ceremonies had faded out by the late Carolingian era. Charles the Bald, grandson of Charlemagne, was interested in learning how the Gallican Mass had been celebrated, and he attended a Mass at which visiting priests from Toledo used the Hispanic rite still current in their own diocese, identical in most respects with the now defunct Gallican ceremonies. Mabillon tells this story as he found it in a letter of Charles that depicts the antiquarian inter-

---

1. P. Salmon, 7 (1944) (xv, xxv, and xcviii). Dom Salmon says that the seventh-century Luxeuil manuscript of the rite shows signs (like corrections and notes) that indicate the lectionary's use in the ninth–tenth centuries, and probably as late as the twelfth–thirteenth centuries, at least in certain parts.

2. Klaus Gamber, *Codices Latini Liturgici Antiquiores*, 2d ed. (Freiburg: Universitätsverlag Freiburg Schweiz, 1968), Part I, pp. 192–93, says that the Gallican rite did not die out everywhere immediately in France; in northern Italy, Gallican customs died out slowly, from about 500 in some places.

ests of a ruler whose own immediate predecessors had suppressed the old rite. When Mabillon himself discovered the Luxeuil Lectionary in the late seventeenth century, the Gallican liturgy was not even a memory. He had to recreate the milieu and the very meaning of the texts with virtually no assistance from the learned world of his day. (*DLG*, Preface and Col. 122.)

Since the documents are so few in French territory, it is necessary to transcend this locale and search for analogues in other areas where the basic characteristics of non-Roman liturgies exist as cognate materials and can fill out the lacunae in the Gallican books. In this quest the Spanish materials are of the greatest importance. Some light is thrown by the Ambrosian (Milanese) and North African records, although neither of these is now considered a Gallic liturgy in the radical sense. The *Gallic* rites, those Western liturgies distinct from the Roman in basic features, comprise the Gallican, Hispanic, Celtic, and possibly the Milanese in its early stages.[3]

As the Spanish liturgical books are the closest analogues to the French, especially in the observance of saints' days, the lectionaries and sacramentaries of the Iberian peninsula are rich testimonials to the practices of Gaul in the sixth to eighth centuries. Here, too, a problem of terminology arises even within the Spanish books themselves. Very often the adjective "Mozarabic" is used as the generic designation for the liturgy of medieval Spain, but it strictly applies only to the centuries from the Moorish invasion of 711 until the imposition of the Roman rite in 1081. Thus it is an imperfect parallel to the Gallican centuries. On the other hand, "Visigothic" is a historical term that roughly matches the French period, as it dates from 589 to 711. The difficulty in using it (just as in using "Mozarabic") lies in the narrowness of its scope, for many features of both the Visi-

---

3. See Rev. Gerard Austin's discussion of the terms "Gallic" and "Gallican" in the introductory chapter to his "Trinitarian Doctrine in the Gallican Liturgy According to the 'Missale Gothicum,'" Diss. Institut Catholique de Paris, 1968, pp. 7–10.

gothic and Mozarabic texts are very old, dating back to the first centuries after the Apostolic conversion of Spain to Christianity. I have chosen to follow a recent trend that applies the word "Hispanic" to the whole liturgical tradition from Apostolic times to the late eleventh century,[4] with the added precaution of giving a date for a text or a custom if it is limited to one phase of Spanish liturgical history.

Editorial interest in providing texts of the Gallican liturgy developed slowly. After the pioneer work of Jean Mabillon, who discovered the *Luxeuil Lectionary* and the *Bobbio Missal*, modern textual analysis began only in the middle of the nineteenth century. First came F. J. Mone's study of ancient Mass formulas, including several Gallican ones.[5] Then two British scholars, John Neale and George Forbes, edited a collection of several texts as *The Ancient Liturgies of the Gallican Church*.[6] Shortly thereafter appeared the seventy-second volume of Migne's *Patrologia*[7] with several Gallican items, including Mabillon's *De Liturgia Gallicana* and his edition of the *Luxeuil Lectionary*, the *Missale Francorum*, and the *Missale Gothicum*. In the early twentieth century the Henry Bradshaw Society included two Gallican texts in its series, the *Bobbio Missal* and the *Missale Gothicum*.[8] The most recent editorial work is that of L. Cunibert Mohlberg in the series

4. This term is the choice of Ángel Fábrega Grau in his edition of the *Pasionario hispanico*, 2 vols. (Madrid–Barcelona: Monumenta Hispaniae Sacra, 1953), as he explains in I, 14. Father Richard Donovan also favors the term "Hispanic" in *The Liturgical Drama in Medieval Spain*, p. 20.

5. These are now commonly referred to as the "Mone Masses." F. J. Mone, *Messen Lateinische und Greichische* (Frankfurt, 1850).

6. (London, 1855–67; rpt. New York: AMS Press, 1970). Although this edition is now superseded by more recent ones, its notes are extremely valuable.

7. (Paris: Garnier Fratres, 1878). A Belgian project to provide modern critical editions of Migne's texts is in progress under the title of *Corpus Christianorum: Series Latina* (Turnhout, Belgium: Brepols, 1953–). An older but still active series of Patristic editions is the *Corpus Scriptorum Ecclesiasticorum Latinorum* (Vindobonae: apud C. Geroldi filium, 1866 to date).

8. *The Bobbio Missal: A Gallican Mass Book*, ed. E. A. Lowe et al. (London: Henry Bradshaw Society, 1917–23), Vols. 53, 58, 61; *A Gallican Sacramentary* (The *Missale Gothicum*), ed. H. M. Bannister (London: Henry Bradshaw Society, 1917), Vols. 52, 54.

known as *Rerum Ecclesiasticarum Documenta*. Here three major Gallican Mass books appear: the *Gothicum*, the *Francorum*, and the *Missale Gallicanum Vetus*,[9] along with several minor texts forming an Appendix (like the so-called "Mone Masses," referred to above).[10] Although several of these service books have in their modern titles the word *missale*, the proper term for an early medieval collection of Mass texts is "sacramentary" (*liber sacramentorum*).[11] The classification of these texts, with their manuscript numbers, original library locations, and modern editions, is the achievement of two European bibliographical works, one in French by Cyrille Vogel[12] and the other in German by Klaus Gamber.[13] It does not seem feasible to reproduce here all of this technical information, especially since condensed versions of it are available in essays by Rev. Johannes Quasten[14] and by Professor Clifford Flanigan.[15]

The sacramentaries are precious repositories of the variable (or proper) prayers in the Gallican Mass, and they shed considerable light on the celebration of saints' days. As I shall consider in a later chapter, they contain a lengthy prayer corresponding to the Roman Preface preceding the Sanctus of the Mass, called the "Contestatio," in which the miracles and heroic suffering of the martyr or confessor are recapitulated from the more lengthy *vita* that might have been read partly during the Matins office

9. *Missale Gothicum*, ed. L. Cunibert Mohlberg (Augsburg: Benno Filser Verlag, 1929); *Missale Francorum*, ed. L. C. Mohlberg (Rome: Herder, 1957); *Missale Gallicanum Vetus*, ed. L. C. Mohlberg, P. Siffrin, and L. Eizenhöfer (Rome: Herder, 1958). The latter two texts are part of the *Rerum Ecclesiasticarum Documenta*, Series Major.

10. The "Mone Masses" are sometimes referred to as the *Missale Richenovense* because the manuscript had been in the possession of the Abbey of Reichenau. See Neale and Forbes, p. vi.

11. See the article "Sacramentaries" in the *New Catholic Encyclopedia* (New York: Harcourt Brace, 1967), XII, 792–800.

12. Vogel, *Introduction aux sources de l'histoire du culte chrétien au moyen âge* (Spoleto: Centro Italiano di Studi sull' Alto Medioevo, n.d. [circa 1965]).

13. Gamber, *Codices*, Part I, pp. 153–193.

14. Quasten, "Gallican Rites," *New Catholic Encyclopedia*, Vol. VI.

15. Flanigan, "The Roman Rite and the Origins of the Liturgical Drama," pp. 263–84.

and partly in the Mass lections. The Collects of the Mass, as well as other prayers, contain allusions, sometimes quite detailed, to the marvelous events of the saint's life, and this kind of adumbration of the *vita* over the whole Mass characterized the Gallican service.[16] It varied from one region to another in an era that knew little of centralized liturgical regulation at levels higher than the diocesan.[17] St. Eulalia's feast day, for example, as it appears in the *Missale Gothicum*, has a "Praefatio" at the beginning of the Mass, in which a direct address to those attending urges them to pray for God's blessing through the intercession of Eulalia and then surveys the story of her martyrdom in considerable detail. This text has no "Contestatio" for her festival. Also in the *Missale Gothicum* the Mass for St. Leudgarius contains an "Immolatio" with a tissue of frequent allusions to his life and martyrdom.[18]

Moreover, the texts that have survived into our day often display a mingling of Gallican customs with those of other contemporary liturgies. The *Bobbio Missal*, for example, was discovered by Mabillon in the north Italian monastery of that name, but does not represent a monastic usage, nor a clearly Italian one. Neale and Forbes regarded it as fundamentally Gallican, probably from the area of France around Luxeuil, and they conjectured that St. Columbanus brought it with him from Luxeuil when he fled to Bobbio.[19] They ventured to "place" it at Besançon, entitling it *Missale Vesontionense* because of an allusion to St. Sigismund of Burgundy. Salmon regards it as contemporary with the Luxeuil Lectionary (seventh century) and of indefinite location in southern France or northern Italy, showing a com-

---

16. Élie Griffe comments that the "Contestatio" contains allusions to the *passiones* of martyrs, but the *libelli* that contained these old prayers have disappeared, leaving only remnants in the missals. (*La Gaule chrétienne*, III, 216.) See the Mass for St. Germain d'Auxerre for a detailed "Collect" of the hagiographical kind, closely related to the "Contestatio," in the *Missale Gallicanum Vetus*, ed. Mohlberg, pp. 3–5.

17. Salmon, VII, lxxvii–lxxviii.

18. *Missale Gothicum*, ed. Neale and Forbes, pp. 69–70, 133–34.

19. Neale and Forbes, p. 205.

plex mingling of Visigothic, Irish, and Roman influences on its Gallican substance.[20] William Porter reverses the proportions, and finds the missal fundamentally Celtic, with Gallican elements.[21]

The type of manuscript in which one would expect to find the saints' lives is not the sacramentary but the lectionary, containing the special readings for the Mass of the day. This is just the point at which the search becomes occluded, however, because in the Gallican lectionary the three readings normally used are Scriptural: the prophetic, apostolic, and evangelical lections (from the Old Testament, New Testament Epistles, and the Gospels). The substitution of a saint's life for the first one or two of these was an extraordinary occurrence, and the *vita* was usually read not from the lectionary but from a separate book, either a *passionarium* for martyrs or a *legendarium* for confessors and virgins. These special collections have survived in very small numbers and have generally appeared in modern editions only as partial extracts. The manuscripts themselves can be located in their European libraries through the bibliographical information supplied by Vogel and Gamber, and a few fragmentary portions have been made available to American readers at the Hill Monastic Library in Minnesota, a film collection of manuscripts being built up at St. John's University.[22] According to A. Fábrega Grau, only the *passionarium* was a liturgical service book; the *legendarium* was a collection for spiritual reading but it was not a regular item in a church's official library.[23] This distinction may account for the scarcity of legendaries and the difficulty of locating them for the Gallican period.

20. Salmon, VII, lxxxv.

21. William S. Porter, *The Gallican Rite* (London: Mowbray, 1958), p. 10. See also the essay by Dom A. Wilmart, "Notice du Missal de Bobbio," in *The Bobbio Missal: A Gallican Mass-Book*, Vol. 61 (1923), pp. 2–58.

22. Dr. Julian G. Plante, Director of this library, indicates that the Hill collection at present contains five fragments of Gallican *passionaria*. They are listed by Gamber under number 278, "Fragmente von Passionaren" (Part I, p. 182), of which St. John's owns microfilms a–g.

23. A. Fábrega Grau, I, 12–13.

There is an abundance of saints' lives in Latin from the early centuries of the Church, many of which were known and copied in the Gallican period, but they do not offer the kind of documentary evidence for public reading in the Divine Office or the Mass that would be so helpful in the present study. Gregory of Tours' hagiography accounts for much of the available material. The *Monumenta Germaniae Historica* contains the work written by him under the title *In Gloria Martyrum*,[24] a series of short, summary narratives stressing miraculous events and comprising more than a thousand *passiones*. It is a kind of encyclopedia that must have been valuable as a reference work for homiletic purposes, but it throws little light on public recitation of the stories; it is unlikely that they were so read. Gregory has also among his minor works a parallel collection of miracles attributed to saints who were not martyrs. This bears the title *Liber in Gloria Confessorum*.[25] In addition, Gregory wrote separate and lengthy *vitae* of St. Andrew, St. Julian, and St. Martin, as well as a *Liber Vitae Patrum* [sic], twenty accounts of bishops, hermits, and abbots.[26]

The *MGH* has also a large number of saints' lives in its series "Scriptores Rerum Merovingicarum," five huge tomes under the caption *Passiones Vitaeque Sanctorum Aevi Merovingici et Antiquiorum Aliquot*, a series that includes many Gallican saints' lives. Wilhelm Levison drew up a "Conspectus" for this ponderous set and placed it at the end of the last volume.[27] It is an admirable bibliographical essay written at the end of the nineteenth century, representing German scholarship at its most meticulous. The essay surveys all the manuscript *codices* from which the saints' lives of these five volumes were drawn for the

---

24. Gregory of Tours, *Miracula et Opera Minora*, ed. Bruno Krusch, *MGH* (Hanover: Hahn, 1885, rpt. 1969). This is Vol. I, pt. 2 of Gregory's *Opera*, the first part an edition of the *Historia Francorum*.
25. Ibid.
26. All of these are edited in this 1969 reprint of the *Miracula et Opera Minora*.
27. *Passiones*. . . . ed. Bruno Krusch (Hanover: Hahn, 1896), Vols. III–VII. Levison's "Prospectus" is in VII, 529–706.

MGH editorial project, and catalogues the legendaries according to date. Although the essay was published in 1896, it remains a valuable guide in an area not covered by the recent bibliographical publications of Vogel and Gamber, which are limited to liturgical texts. Few of the extant manuscript collections are of the Gallican era; few, indeed, dated before the eleventh century, even when saintly subjects of the *vitae* are well-known Gallican leaders like Caesarius of Arles or St. Germain d'Auxerre. Levison indicates that the oldest of the *codices* is MS Paris 9550 of the seventh century, containing the account of the "Acaunensium martyrum" written by Eucherius, bishop of Lyon in the fifth century, and known to have been read publicly in the early sixth century.[28]

When we have studied the Gallican liturgical texts, we can and should turn to the Hispanic liturgy for comparable source materials in the Visigothic era, roughly contemporary with the sixth-to-eighth-century span of the French materials. Here one meets the term "Mozarabic" in the titles of most editorial projects, but as previously explained the Visigothic period is also encompassed by the designation and should usually be regarded as embraced by the texts unless special exception is stated. In the early twentieth century a major editorial enterprise was undertaken in the *Monumenta Ecclesiae Liturgica*, based in Paris. Two of its volumes contain editions made by the Benedictine scholar Marius Férotin: *Le 'Liber Ordinum' en usage dans l'église wisigothique et mozarabe d'Espagne*[29] and *Le 'Liber mozarabicus sacramentorum' et les manuscrits mozarabes*.[30] The *Liber Ordinum* contains the ritual for ordinations, consecrations, blessings, and so on, as well as the special Holy Week ceremonies and many votive Masses of various kinds. The *Liber Sacramentorum* contains the Mass prayers of the liturgical year, exclusive

---

28. Ibid., V, 529, and III, 24.   29. (Paris: Firmin-Didot, Vol. 5, 1904).
30. (Paris: Firmin-Didot, Vol. 6, 1912).

of any lectionary materials, and therefore does not itself include saints' lives.

The Masses in this Spanish rite contain a prayer comparable to the "Contestatio" of the Gallican service, but it is here called the "Inlatio" or "Illatio." It corresponds in its position to the "Preface" of the Roman Mass, and on saints' days could be a quite lengthy recapitulation of hagiographical material. Like the Gallican Mass, the Hispanic celebration of a sanctoral feast was permeated with allusions to the *vita*. In Chapter III below, a discussion of the "Inlatio" for the feasts of St. Clement and St. Martin illustrates this form of Spanish devotion.

Work on the liturgical lectionaries began in 1893 with Dom Germain Morin's edition of the *liber commicus* from the great monastery of Silos.[31] This strange term *commicus* is the one used in the Spanish liturgy for an anthology of readings, and appears under different spellings that indicate confusion about its original sense.[32] Morin's edition was based on the manuscript in the Bibliothèque Nationale of Paris (MS. N. A. lat. 2171). More recently, a critical edition of the five surviving versions of the *liber commicus* appeared in mid-century, edited by Fray Justo Perez de Urbel, using as basic text MS. 35-8 of the Cathedral of Toledo and collating Toledo 35-4, along with Silos (as above), León (Cod. 2) and San Millán de la Cogolla (Cod. Emil. 22).[33] Like the Gallican lectionary of Luxeuil, the book contains the Scriptural readings from the Old Testament, Pauline epistles, and the Gospels, but the different versions also contain a few saints' lives

31. *Liber Commicus sive Lectionarium Missae quo Toletana Ecclesia ante Annos Mille et Ducentos Utebatur. Anecdota Maredsolana* I (Maredsous: Desclée, De Brouwer, 1893).

32. The proper spelling would be *liber commatus*, says Fray Justo Perez, for a book of selections or fragments. It was often referred to as *liber comitis*, the book being regarded as a "companion" for a priest traveling, e.g., through a large rural parish. See the following note 33, with reference to pp. xiv–xv of Vol. II.

33. *Liber Commicus*, ed. Fray Justo Perez de Urbel and Atilano Gonzalez y Ruiz-Zorrilla, 2 vols. (Madrid: C. Bermejo, 1950–55). (These are Volumes 2 and 3 of the *Monumenta Hispaniae Sacra: Series Liturgica*.)

used to supplement or replace the normal type of readings. Fray Justo does not print all of these special lections, but he does give the account of the miracles associated with St. Stephen, a lection that appears in the Silos manuscript (under December 26). It is actually a well-known extract from Augustine's *De Civitate Dei*, Book 22. Fray Justo refers to other saints' lives in the *codices* without reproducing their texts, most of them extracts from works available elsewhere, like the account of St. Helena's discovery of the true Cross, taken from Eusebius' *Historia Ecclesiastica*, and appearing in the León *liber commicus.*

The Hispanic churches kept a special lectionary for accounts of the martyrs, to be used in place of the readings in the *liber commicus* on their festivals. As indicated above, this type of book, called a *pasionario*, was a regular component of a church's official liturgical library, as a *legendario* was not.[34] Two versions of this book have survived, in the manuscripts of Cardeña and of Silos. Approximately twenty-five *passiones* are included in the critical edition of these manuscripts made in 1953–55, by A. Fábrega Grau.[35] The miracles of St. Stephen, mentioned above as appearing in the *Liber Commicus* of Silos, form part of the *Pasionario* collection in an abridged form of the Augustinian extract.[36] The narrative of SS. Julian and Basilissa, which figures so prominently in the Luxeuil Lectionary, occurs in the *Pasionario* as well.[37] This story, which had appeared in Spain early in the Visigothic era and was introduced into Gaul in the seventh century,[38] is almost a symbol of Hispanic–Gallican relationships in hagiographical literature.

A study of all these texts, and of other fragmentary ones scattered in minor editions and commentaries, provides evidence that the public recitation of saints' lives is indicated there in the

---

34. Fábrega Grau, *Pasionario hispanico,* I, 12–13.
35. Ibid.
36. Ibid., II, 78–83.
37. See P. Salmon's discussion of the relationship between the Gallican and Spanish versions (*Le Lectionnaire de Luxeuil,* VII, lxxvi.
38. Fábrega Grau, I, 202–3.

service books and that the evidence supplements the scattered allusions made by ecclesiastics, poets, and historians of the Merovingian and Frankish eras. The sacramentaries and lectionaries, although often showing lacunae in crucial passages, reveal not only the practice of substituting the saint's life in place of ordinary Scriptural lections, but also the radiation of allusions to the marvelous events and heroic sufferings throughout the entire sanctoral liturgy. Where a Gallican text proves inadequate, a comparable prayer formula or lection in the Hispanic rite can serve to illuminate the uncertainty and solidify the evidence. With a sketch of the bibliographical resources such as given in the present chapter, one can turn to the dramatic tradition behind the texts themselves for the implementation of the general lines of thought marked out, converging on the public recitation of the saint's *vita* as essentially a dramatic performance. Here there appears to be a tradition of late Roman theater, the mime as creative *mimesis* in a complex of recitative, music, and liturgical dance.

CHAPTER III

THE TRADITION OF ROMAN DRAMA AND THE SAINT'S LIFE

The scarcity and the expense of manuscripts throughout the Middle Ages, even in affluent periods, severely limited the accessibility of texts and created a long tradition of public gatherings for all kinds of reading—instructive, inspiring, and entertaining. This is true not only for the early periods like the Merovingian, but even for the very late eras of relative sophistication, in the courtly literary circles of France and England, as in Chaucer's day.[1] Although Erich Auerbach has expressed the opinion that a literary public in Western Europe ceased to exist from the fifth to the eleventh centuries, he nevertheless recognized that the vernacular languages during these dark centuries developed oral literatures that were recited or read to people of all classes, educated and illiterate.[2] Auerbach himself, however, underestimated the role of *liturgical* reading, with its accompanying visual splendor and musical beauty, in the creation of a European culture that was more than simply verbal, more than literary. The complexity of the recited narrative, read or chanted in a style of performing artistry, is an early medieval phenomenon, with roots in classical Rome. To this historical perspective Jean Mabillon makes no direct contribution, but the material of

1. One of the comic dimensions of Chaucer's work, as is well known, is the discrepancy between the authorial *persona* as portrayed in his works and the reader-reciter of them as a familiar public figure at the court.

2. *Literary Language and its Public in Late Latin Antiquity and in the Middle Ages*, tr. Ralph Manheim (New York: Pantheon Books, 1965), pp. 23, 252, 261 et passim.

his essays opens up vistas into a historical continuity that has not been really grasped. Although the task of linking the Christian liturgical reading with the pagan classical theater is a complicated one, it rests upon the relation of Roman theatrical performance itself to a tradition of formal public reading.[3]

The whole problem of continuity involves a definition of literary and musical *form*, and a redefinition of drama itself for the late classical and the medieval periods. We need to reassess drama in terms other than the imitation of an action as commonly understood, and in categories less rigid than those usually imposed by the school of Karl Young. This must be done, however, without destroying the boundary between liturgy and art, as present-day theories of "Rezeptionsästhetik" tend to do. In confronting these two schools of thought, one finds that both of them deny to the early Christian centuries the concept of drama itself and an understanding of ancient Roman theatrical art. The Young–Frank coterie and the Konstanz school of Rezeptionsästhetik (including Clifford Flanigan in the United States) form a strange partnership when their views are juxtaposed, but on theoretical and practical grounds they draw the same conclusions. The response lies in the tradition of voice and address in antiquity, and its relationship to drama. We can deal first with theory of drama and then with the practice of pantomimic art on the stage.

The position that Grace Frank took on the early Christian comprehension of Roman drama occurs in her opening chapter of *Medieval French Drama:* "It is evident from the testimony of countless medieval writers that the works of Terence and Plautus were not connected in their minds with any idea of the impersonation of actors speaking upon a stage, that the very

---

3. I sketched out the general plan of my theory on the Gallican relationship to medieval drama against a background of previous scholarship in an essay published as "French Medievalists and the Saint's Play: A Problem for American Scholarship," *Medievalia et Humanistica*, New Series (1975), 51–62. Here I am developing one aspect, that of public reading or recitative.

meaning of the word 'drama' was misunderstood, and that the terms 'comedy' and 'tragedy' were regularly misapplied throughout the Middle Ages to narrative and even to lyrical forms of literature. . . ."[4] This apparent misconception, however, may be a transformation, so that medieval theory accurately reproduces a living theatrical tradition. The whole character of Roman dramatic art in late antiquity and in the early Middle Ages was symbolic rather than representational, and it is this fact that governs the medieval practice, not a confusion of genres or forms. Plays with full representational activity gradually disappeared from the Roman world, ceding to a symbolic mode of gesture and rhythmic movement, accompanied by recitation or commentary to guarantee an intelligible narrative line to the spectators.

Frank attributes this medieval confusion about ancient drama to the Latin grammarians of late antiquity from the fourth century on, and to their imitators: Servius, Diomedes, Donatus, Isidore of Seville and Bede.[5] Hans Jauss takes the same view.[6] The grammarians make a classification of poetry (*poema, poematos*) into three kinds according to the voices speaking in each type: one in which only the poet speaks, another in which only characters speak (without intervention by the poet), and finally a mixed type in which the poet serves as basic voice but introduces passages of quoted dialogue by the characters (as in epic). Frank finds confusion here because Servius, commenting on Vergil's *Eclogues*, seems to define bucolic poetry as drama. She sees Diomedes doing the same.[7] This would put the eclogues

4. Frank, *The Medieval French Drama*, p. 6.
5. Ibid., pp. 6–7.
6. Jauss, "Theory of Genres," p. 96. He cites Ernst Curtius, *European Literature and the Latin Middle Ages*, tr. Willard Trask (Princeton, N.J.: Princeton University Press, 1967, Exkursus V); also Edgar de Bruyne, *Études d'esthétique médiévale*, 3 vols. (Brugge: De Tempel, 1946), II, 18 ff.
7. Frank, pp. 6–7. The passage in Servius is quite misleading because he found all three of the voice-structures distributed throughout the Vergilian eclogues. (Servius, *Commentarii*, ed. Thilo and Hagen [Lipsiae: Teubner, 1887], III, 29–30).

into the same category as tragedy and comedy. Jauss, too, reacts negatively,[8] but I think that both of them are misreading the texts here. There is no confusion in the division because the grammarians are not defining genres or "forms" of delivery[9] but dividing poetry itself into modes or forms of voice structure.

This classification of poetry was not a superficial one and it was much older than the Latin grammarians of the fourth century A.D., as Craig La Drière stated in an essay on "Voice and Address," and as Ernst Curtius has recognized.[10] The classification goes back to Plato and Aristotle, and La Drière observed that it was thoroughly understood and used throughout antiquity.[11] Diomedes, of the fourth century, was the most precise and accurate of the grammarians in articulating the theory of *poema*, which he specifically attributed to Greek origins: "Poematos genera sunt tria, aut enim activum est vel imitativum, quod Graeci *dramaticon* vel *mimeticon*, aut enarrativum vel enuntiativum, quod Graeci *exegeticon* vel *apangelticon* dicunt, aut commune vel mixtum, quod Graeci *koinon* vel *mikton* appellant."[12] The crucial term for the present problem is the category of *dramaticon*, which Diomedes goes on to define: "*Dramaticon* est vel activum in quo personae agunt solae sine ullius poetae interlocutione, ut se habent tragicae et comicae fabulae."[13] In a still further analysis of the dramatic category, he is more explicit. He

8. Jauss, "Theory of Genres," p. 96.

9. This is Jauss' term, ibid.

10. La Drière, "Voice and Address," in *Dictionary of World Literature: Criticism—Forms—Techniques*, ed. Joseph Shipley, rev. ed. (New York: Philosophical Library, 1953, repr. 1968), p. 442; see also Curtius, *European Literature*, p. 440, for a sensitive discussion of the problem of voice in antiquity. David Hult, although he does not deal with the Gallican era, has an excellent article on the distinction between *mimesis* and mime. ("The Limits of Mimesis: Notes Toward a Generic Revision of Medieval Theater," *L'Esprit Créateur*, 23 (1983), 49–63.

11. The Platonic discussion of the tripartite division is in *The Republic*, III, 392D–394C, and the Aristotelian version occurs in *The Poetics*, 1448a20–24. (La Drière, ibid.)

12. Diomedes, "De Poematibus," *Ars Grammatica*, Book III, in *Grammatici Latini*, ed. Heinrich Keil, 7 vols. (Lipsiae: Teubner, 1855–80), I, 482.

13. Ibid.

has a paragraph to which he gives the caption, "De Generibus Poematos Dramatici Vel Activi," and he says: "Poematos dramatici vel activi genera sunt quattuor, apud Graecos tragica comica satyrica mimica, apud Romanos praetextata tabernaria Atellana planipes."[14] The mime is specifically named as fourth in this *activum* mode. The four categories constitute ancient drama, but he goes on to provide for another cognate species— dialogue without action in some of Vergil's eclogues: "quo genere [activum] scripta est prima bucolicon et ea cuius initium est 'quo te, Moeri, pedes?'"[15] *Dramatic poetry,* is, then, the *genus,* with two species, (1) *drama* (with action accompanying speech, as in tragedy, comedy, satyr play, and mime) and (2) poetic dialogue.

The place of the eclogue in poetic classification is not the relevant issue here. Modern literary scholars like Frank, Curtius, Jauss, de Bruyne, and Behrens have puzzled over the terminology used by the grammarians,[16] and these theorists of the fourth to eighth centuries may indeed have caused confusion among later theorists, up to the twelfth century, at least. The nature of drama itself, however, was clearly understood by them, and seen as a tradition from ancient Rome. Diomedes is unambiguous: "Dramata autem dicuntur tragica aut comica παρὰ τὸ δρᾶν, id est agere. Latine fabulae appellantur sive fatibulae; in Latinis enim fabulis plura sunt cantica quae canuntur:

14. Ibid.   15. Ibid.
16. Edgar de Bruyne and also Irene Behrens present a key to these difficult passages, recognizing that Diomedes understood the classical tradition and took action for granted in drama, not in dialogued poems. In de Bruyne's words: "D'après Diomède, le genre dramatique appelé aussi mimétique, imitatif, actif, comprend cinq espèces principales: la tragédie, la comédie, le drame satirique, la pantomime et des poèmes du type de certaines églogues." (*Études d' esthétique médiévale,* I, 101.) Note that he uses the word "poèmes" for the eclogues, not "drames." Behrens' discussion is less clear, but she says that certain eclogues belong in the category of the dramatic, because of their structuring of voice patterns. (*Die Lehre von der Einteilung der Dichtkunst* [Halle/Saale: Max Niemeyer, 1940], p. 27.

vel [assuredly] a faciendo; nam et agi fabula non referri [re-counted] ab actoribus dicitur. ideoque Horatius utraque signifi-catione interpretatur, cum ita de fabula dicit, 'aut agitur res in scenis aut acta refertur,' sicut in choro."[17]

Isidore of Seville[18] and the Venerable Bede[19] continue to work with these categories, without evidence of confusion or uncertainty. De Bruyne comments that the Irish and Anglo-Saxon scholars from the sixth to the ninth centuries knew well this tradition of the Late Latin grammarians.[20] Thus we can say that the comprehension of ancient drama survived into and beyond the period of the Gallican liturgy with which I am concerned. Isidore's discussion is directly indebted to Servius' passage, while Bede (without mentioning his source) gives a nearly verbatim reproduction of Diomedes' "tria genera" paragraph. He makes this section XXV the culmination of his whole treatise, *De Arte Metrica*, as a kind of flourish. Having reproduced Diomedes' classification (see above), he adds some Biblical examples to the classical ones, notably the *Cantica Canticorum* in the category of dramatic poetry, as comparable to the classical eclogues.[21] His definition of the *dramaticon* (activum) class reads a little differently from Diomedes' in the final sentence: "*Dramaticon est uel actiuum in quo personae loquentes introducuntur sine poetae interlocutione, ut se habent tragoediae et fabulae (drama enim Latine fabula dicitur.)*"[22]

17. Diomedes, p. 490.

18. Isidore, *Etymologiae*, VIII, 7, ed. W. M. Lindsay, 2 vols. (Oxford: Clarendon Press, 1911).

19. Bede, *De Arte Metrica*, Sect. XXV, in *Corpus Christianorum*, ed. C. B. Kendall and M. H. King (Typographi Brepols Turnholti, 1975), Vol. 123A.

20. De Bruyne makes this observation in the shortened form of his *Études*, translated into English by Eileen Hennessy as *The Esthetics of the Middle Ages* (New York: Frederick Ungar, 1969), p. 39.

21. Bede, p. 140.

22. Ibid., pp. 139–140. De Bruyne notices the word *fabula* as the Latin term for drama, and cites Varro, *De Lingua Latina*, VI, 55 and 77, as a background for this usage by Bede. (*Études*, I, 100–101.) However, the tradition is surely not tied simply to Varro's linguistic speculations, for *fabula* had been one of the terms for

In summary, the classification of drama, for which the Latin language had the traditional word *fabula,* was a species of dramatic poetry, itself one of three characters or modes of poetry. The conception of mime as recitative with silent activity, then, finds its place as the fourth in the general category of dramatic poetry, that is, within the *activum* type. Having dealt with theory of drama, as understood in antiquity and in the early Middle Ages, we can turn to its practice, specifically in the popular tradition of the Roman pantomime. This tradition, too, continues into the Gallican era, and can be regarded as a "horizon of expectation" even in modern Deconstructionist terms. Moreover, the liturgical drama of the early medieval period should be placed somehow in this tradition of mimetic performance, depending on voice structure and using costume, gesture, and scenic effects.

There is well-established evidence from Roman history to support such a thesis. The level of Roman taste in theatrical entertainment was never very elevated or refined, even in periods when it could be served by a superior dramatist like Terence or Seneca. Although Rome had from time to time great comedy and tragedy that were worthy derivatives of the Hellenic Greek theater, its own perennial interests were in more primitive and rude forms of entertainment like athletic combats, the dance, and pantomime. Terence himself complained in his *Hecyra* of the low-level competition that his sophisticated art of comedy had to encounter.[23] For centuries the popular mode of Atellan farce rivalled the formal art of high comedy, and the *fabulae salticae* or pantomimic dances vied with the performance of tragic drama.[24] Historians of the theater commonly record a decline of

---

a *play* in Classical Latin. (*Oxford Latin Dictionary,* I, 665.) (See above, Ch. I, n. 38, for the meaning of "conversation" as *fabula.*)

23. Gilbert Norwood, *The Art of Terence* (1923), (New York: Russell and Russell, 1965), pp. 2–3.

24. Bieber, *The History of the Greek and Roman Theater,* 2nd ed. (Princeton, N.J.: Princeton University Press, 1961), p. 165; George Duckworth, *The Nature of Roman Comedy* (Princeton, N.J.: Princeton University Press, 1952), pp. 71–72.

Roman dramatic art in the Empire into lower forms of entertainment,[25] but these inferior types had long been there in the ancient Latin world, easily drawing large audiences in the city and the town. Then at the rise of the Empire they simply triumphed over the more intellectual and literary rival represented by stage plays, and they prevailed until the collapse of the Roman world itself.

In the Silver Age of Roman culture, therefore, public entertainment was more and more conformed to the popular taste for drama of a freer, less structured type than the genuine stage play. The mime, the pantomime, and the Atellan farce were the favored genres, all of them possessing a substitute for a plot design and enacted roles. All of them, too, required some kind of basic voice or "choral" voice to control the performance and prevent its disintegration into merely fragmented, incidental, or unintelligible lines and gestures. The element of improvisation had a large place in these dramatic genres, with satire upon political and social life developing *ad hoc* in a Saturnalian spirit of freedom, especially in the Atellan farce and the mime. The voice of a narrator or commentator provided a unifying point of departure and a recurrent guide through the hilarity, bitterness, or gravity of the story line, and this basic voice served as the principle of structure insofar as the entertainment achieved rational order and aesthetic coherence.

The pantomime, as it occurred in late antiquity, affords the best illustration of a theatrical entertainment embodying the above elements of drama and differing in structure from a "play." Bieber describes it in these terms: "The pantomime actor danced the individual roles, which means that he had to refine his gestures to such a high degree and perform his movements so expressively that in him alone one could see embodied now a god, now a goddess, now a hero, and now a heroine. These

25. J. Wight Duff, *Literary History of Rome in the Silver Age,* 2nd ed. (London: E. Benn, 1960), pp. 273–78.

characters were made more readily distinguishable by changes in the actor's masks and attributes."[26] Plot line is developed by a collective *persona* or an individual narrator and the actions needed to implement the "plot" are handled symbolically by the pantomimic performer, who passes successively through a series of roles. Together the chorus and the single *pantomimus* create drama, fictively projecting a number of impersonated characters involved in the unfolding of a story. Professor Young's definition of drama is here fulfilled in a way that he would probably not have accepted as valid, but for which there is a strong and solid historical basis.

In a dramatic performance of this relatively flexible type, in which the voice structure is centrally important, the artistry of the presentation is a highly embellished vocal sophistication. The beauty of the trained voice—reciting or singing—becomes the source of fascination and enjoyment above all other elements present. There is an almost hypnotic effect in a great voice, and its power in charming and holding attention is crucial when spectacle and action are in abeyance. A law of compensation seems to be operative here, in which vocal richness achieves an exceptional intensity in order to balance the thinness of plot texture. The skill of the *recitator* or singer was the artistic basis of the Roman theatrical tradition rather than histrionic ability or visual craftsmanship on the stage. It does not matter whether the voice is reading a text of Terence that had originally been written for the legitimate theater, or whether it is commenting on the silent ballet of a skilled pantomimic dancer. It matters only that the person recites, reads, or sings beautifully, with a sonorous resonance and technical virtuosity that can move the hearts of an audience.

If the presence of genuine drama in this tradition of recitative is recognized for the final centuries of the Roman era, a way is thereby cleared for an understanding of dramatic recitative in

26. Bieber, p. 235.

the early medieval liturgy. More precisely, a special significance emerges for the Matins lections and Mass readings in the liturgy. There have been many attempts to link the medieval religious drama with ancient Latin and Greek theater by associating it somehow with the secular acting tradition. The scholarly controversies generated by the problem have been heated ones, and the case for a confluence of the pagan and Christian mimetic practices has generally been an inconclusive one, principally because texts are scarce for the documentation of the view.[27] However, the texts that witness to the continuity of ancient and medieval theater are, in Western Europe, the Gallican saints' lives. These religious readings, chanted as recitative, imitate not the substance of ancient plays or mimes (Heaven forbid!), but rather the techniques of delivery, voice structure, and symbolic narrative line that were embedded in the pagan Roman theatrical tradition.

The Gallican experiments of this kind, however, were not the earliest ones and must be viewed as manifestations of a process operative at one time or another and in various ways in the Patristic era of Christianity, notably in the Eastern Mediterranean, from the fourth century onward. This phenomenon has been reconstructed by historians from scattered records in the East, first Syriac and later Byzantine. The Roman mime, nevertheless, is central to the process. The principle involved is usually called the *contrafactum*, although the Spaniards have coined a phrase of their own denoting the change: *a lo divino*. The best study of the process is that of Bruce Wardropper, but the focus of his book is narrow, restricted to the poetic and musical text. His title indicates this: *Historia de la poesía lírica a lo divino en la cristiandad occidental*.[28] Wardropper recognizes that the process can take

---

27. The literature of this controversy can be sampled in Chambers, I, 1–41; Benjamin Hunningher, *The Origin of the Theater, passim*. I have found of special value the work of Adolfo Bonilla y San Martin, *Las Bacantes o del origen de teatro* (Madrid: Rivadeneyra, 1921).

28. (Madrid: Revista de Occidente, 1958).

place in literary themes of many kinds, and can also be operative in activities like preaching or entertaining, but the form of
the mutation *par excellence* uses the song or lyric poem. He considers the earliest experiment on record to be the achievement
of St. Ephraim in the fourth century,[29] although the heretic
Arius is said to have successfully made dramatic use of pagan
mimic techniques for pedagogical purposes a century earlier.[30]

The principle of the *contrafactum* or sacralization of the pagan
seems to have been operative in large, sweeping ways at first.
Ephraim, the Syrian, and some others belonging to his era were
at pains to make use of well-known musical elements in pagan
religious worship and simply adapt them to Christian circumstances. He gathered choirs of virgins dedicated to religious life
and had them trained to sing hymns in public church services
on high feast days, especially of martyrs. Christian converts
were familiar with feminine choruses in ancient rites and were
attached to the practice,[31] for example, as it was being used by
heretical teachers (Bardesanes and Harmonicus). Ephraim himself composed Syriac hymns, from which the dramatic homilies
(*kontakia*) were later developed by the sixth century *mélodes*,
above all by the great Romanos.[32] Other sweeping claims for
transformations of the secular are more obscure and controversial, such as the notion that Western plain chant was an imitation of popular secular melodies;[33] but into such thorny problems we cannot enter here.

Specific transformations were often connected with the cele-

29. Wardropper, pp. 84–85.

30. Cottas, pp. 60–62; Lindsay, *Byzantium into Europe*, p. 314.

31. Johannes Quasten, *Music and Worship in Pagan and Christian Antiquity*, tr.
Boniface Ramsey (Washington: National Association of Pastoral Musicians,
1983), pp. 76–79, 169. The English translation is based on the second edition
of the German text, *Musik und Gesang in den Kulten der heidnischen Antike und
Christlichen Frühzeit* (Münster: Aschendorff, 1973).

32. Archdale King, *The Rites of Eastern Christendom*, 2 vols. 1947 (New York:
AMS Reprint, 1972), I, 121.

33. Wardropper, pp. 90ff.

bration of a martyr's feast, from at least this fourth century. Here the underlying substratum was the institution known as the *pervigilium*, the all-night vigil in honor of a pagan god. Again, it was a case of Christian neophytes clinging to an older form of devotion or celebration and church authorities making a reluctant compromise. Father Quasten has portrayed the unstable and perilous temporizing represented by this ecclesiastical decision, a tradition that Augustine of Hippo was to deplore and to criticize in his own day, about the end of the fourth century.

The *pervigilium* was originally a pagan Greek custom under the name of *Pannuchides*, with which music, dance, and song were often associated.[34] Sophocles, for example, gives casual testimony to the practice in his tragedy of *Antigone*, where the first choral ode of the play concludes with an invitation to Theban citizens that they celebrate their recent victory over the sons of Oedipus: "Let us enjoy forgetfulness after the late wars, and visit all the temples of the gods with night-long dance and song; and may Bacchus be our leader, whose dancing shakes the land of Thebes."[35] The tenacity of Christian converts in their affection for such ritual must have been a constant problem in the early Church, leading to the establishment of vigils preparing for the feasts of martyrs. Some prominent leaders, like Basil of Caesarea, defended the practice; St. Ephraim, while permitting it, cautioned his congregation to defer the festive celebration until after the religious ceremony.[36] One striking piece of testimony, coming from approximately 360, reveals an untroubled acceptance of this kind of celebration. It is a sermon for the feast of St. Polyeuctus, connected with an unidentified Eastern church, and is the *pièce de résistance* in surviving documentation.

This sermon was edited by Benjamin Aubé in its original

34. Quasten, *Music and Worship*, pp. 169–70.
35. Tr. by R. C. Jebb and reprinted in *Greek Drama*, ed. Moses Haddas (New York: Bantam Books, 1982), p. 85.
36. Quasten, *Music and Worship*, p. 175.

Greek text and in an early medieval Latin translation, probably of the fifth or sixth century.[37] The homilist invites his congregation to enter into the spirit of the celebration: "In ejus honorem, si placet, ut fieri solet, tripudiabimus, et ad ejus historiam pertinentia facta in memoriam revocabimus, ita ut, fixis in memoriam beatis ejus dictis, sanctissimae ejus memoriae, secundum Scripturas, fiamus participes animosque nostros in vera fide confirmare possimus" (p. 79). Polyeuctus is the subject of a commemoration consisting in a review of his deeds and his words and the incorporation of them into some kind of sacred dance to which the people are accustomed. The verb *tripudiabimus* renders the Greek *Choreusomen*, which Aubé translates (p. 20) by the French noun *choeurs* (an ambivalent term for song or dance) but which Prosper Alfaric translates as *nos danses;* J. Quasten renders it as *unsere gewohnten Tänze*, and Ramsey as "our customary dances."[38]

In the Latin West the vigil services and celebrations for martyrs came under the same principle of the *contrafactum* for justification, but in some views, especially those of Augustine, they invited strong censure. Writing to Bishop Alypius of Tagaste in 395, Augustine deplored the permission that had been given in earlier times for the martyrs' vigils, and expressed disapproval of abuses that had grown up in relation to these festivities, especially drunkenness.[39] In one of his five sermons on St. Cyprian martyr, Augustine inveighed against the custom, noting that the very locale of Cyprian's tomb was the haunt of dancers: "istum tam sanctum locum . . . invaserat pestilentia et petulantia saltatorum."[40] Vénétia Cottas observes about this passage in

37. Aubé, *Polyeucte dans l'histoire* (Paris: Firmin-Didot, 1882), pp. 40–41 and 72.

38. Alfaric, *Chanson*, II, 75; Quasten, *Musik und Gesang*, pp. 243–44; Ramsey, p. 175.

39. Augustine, *Ep.* 29, 8–9 (*Corpus Scriptorum Ecclesiasticorum Latinorum*, 34, 119, 6).

40. Augustine, *Sermo* cccxi, "In Natali Cypriani Martyris," ed. Migne, *PL*, Vol. 38, col. 1415.

Augustine that it gives reason to infer the playing of mimed dramas in churches as early as the fourth century.[41] The passage may not support that strong an interpretation, but it is significant that during the last decade of the century the Third Council of Carthage was promulgating regulations about the public reading of saints' lives in churches, as we shall see below (Chapter V). J. Quasten cites not only this Council of Carthage, but also two earlier ones (Elvira, 300, and Laodicea, c. 360) as condemning the practices of the martyrs' vigils.[42] The other side of the coin, however, is that Paulinus of Nola sponsored well-known and highly respected vigil services for St. Felix of an orderly kind, and that Sidonius Apollinaris recorded his experience of a laudable vigil service for St. Just that he attended in the Gaul of his day.[43]

The kind of dance and music associated with the vigils is not always clearly depicted in the allusions, but the essential point to be made about them is their relationship to the tradition of mime. Only in this association can one trace the continuity of the custom. The phenomenon, I think, is not a distinction between *Feier* and *Spiel*, in the recently developed terminology of Walter Lipphardt and his associates,[44] but rather the highlighting of stylized movement and gesture in a symbolic pattern that projects a narrative. It is the absorption of a pagan custom into a Christian framework in which neither the old nor the new is clearly *Feier* (ritual) or *Spiel* (a play), but rather *ludus* in the generic philosophical sense of "play," to use the terminology of Johan Huizinga.[45]

---

41. Cottas, p. 62.
42. Quasten, *Music and Worship*, p. 176.
43. Ibid., p. 174.
44. Lipphardt, *Lateinische Osterfeiern und Osterspiele*, 7 vols. (Berlin and New York: De Gruyter, 1975–83). Helmut de Boor, *Die Textgeschichte der lateinischen Osterfeiern* (Tübingen: Niemayer, 1967), pp. 1–27; Clifford Flanigan, "The Fleury Playbook," pp. 361–2.
45. Huizinga, *Homo Ludens: A Study of the Play Element in Culture* (New York: Roy Publishers, 1950), pp. 18–19 and all of Ch. II.

The backdrop for the *contrafactum* as mimic performance is therefore Eastern, as the Byzantinists claim. I am not here attempting a study of the primary documents, because I regard the case as one already made by specialists in the field of Eastern musicology. The Byzantine mime is recognized as a late reimposition of the Roman mime upon Eastern culture, and this Christianized form of acting and recitative has the Roman exemplar as its ultimate model, both in the East and in the West.[46] This form became also the Gallican experiment of the sixth century, in my judgment, whether the model was immediately present in Romanized Gaul or was transmitted by way of a Byzantine influence on the Gallican liturgy.[47] The route of transmission will probably never be perfectly clear, because the mimic practice was endemic in the life of the whole Mediterranean world. The presumption of an Eastern origin for the Christianization is heavily weighted with probability, however, because of the much higher general level of culture in the early Byzantine Empire than in the war-torn areas of Gaul and Spain in the era of Visigothic invasion and settlement.

Byzantinists in the earlier half of our century were caught in a dilemma of terminology and definition, so that a forceful case for drama in the Eastern liturgy could not be made and was not generally accepted. La Piana and Cottas were engaged in a controversy over the interpretation of the historical records, but both of them recognized the use of mimic techniques in the churches, Cottas opting for a pervasive use of them throughout the liturgy from the fourth century onwards, La Piana being much more reserved and cautious about speculations of this sort. Each has a general statement indicating how far to go in this direction.

46. See Introduction.
47. The relationship of the Gallican liturgy to Eastern rites has long been a highly controversial subject. See Father J. Quasten's "Gallican Rites," *NCE*, VI, 258; and Gabriel Coless, O.S.B., "Recent Liturgical Study," *American Benedictine Review*, 22 (1971), 395; É. Griffe, "Aux Origines de la liturgie gallicane," *Bulletin de la littérature ecclésiastique de Toulouse*, 52 (1951), 17–43.

Cottas, referring to the fourth century, A.D.:

Une fois la gesticulation mimique généralisée dans l'Eglise [sic], elle s'introduisit dans toute composition liturgique, soit acclamative, soit psalmique, dans toute lecture sainte ou dans toute autre partie de l'office à l'exemple des offices d'Alexandrie. . . .

(p. 64)

And La Piana:

Riassumendo: *l'omelia narrativa* è la culla del drama sacro; nell'omelia il drama si sviluppa gradatamente, e, aiutato dall'azione liturgica, commincia ad assumere anche qualche forma esteriore di azione dramatica, e via scende dall'ambone nel coro e nella nave. Accanto alla omelia dramatica si è intanto sviluppato un genere che ha con essa delle affinità: il *cantico sacro*, anch' esso di indole narrativa e dramatica e dipendente a sua volta per la forma dalle mimodie profane. Sotto l'influsso in parte della letteratura siriaca, e molto più sotto l'impulso delle naturali esigenze del gusto dramatico, acuito dal bisogno di opporre un spettaculo cristiano al Mimo licenzioso, l'omelia dramatica e il cantico sacro si fondono gradatamente in un solo componimento, formando il drama sacro poetico della letteratura bizantina, prototipo di tutte le rappresentazioni sacre delle letterature cristiane posteriori.

(Le Rappresentazioni, p. 58)[48]

The two Byzantinists were at odds not over the existence of the *contrafactum* but over its extent and influence. La Piana, reviewing Cottas' book of 1931, long after the appearance of his own 1912 monograph, was harsh on what he saw as exaggeration.[49] She saw "mimodic" techniques everywhere in the liturgy, while he hedged his generalizations with statements that withdrew what he seemed to be granting. In spite of this controversy, both

---

48. La Piana is saying: The narrative homily is the cradle of sacred drama; in the homily drama is developed step by step, and, aided by the liturgical action, it begins to take on also some form of external dramatic action and speedily comes down from the ambo into the choir and into the nave. Alongside the dramatic homily there is meanwhile developed a genre which has some affinity with it: sacred song, even this of a nature narrative and dramatic and dependent in its turn on the structure of secular mime. Under the influence in part of Syriac literature, and much more under the impact of the natural demands of dramatic taste, stimulated by the need to oppose a Christian type of show to the scurrilous Mime, the dramatic homily and sacred song are molded into a single composition gradually, forming the sacred poetic drama of Byzantine literature, prototype of all the religious drama of the later Christian literatures.

49. La Piana, "The Byzantine Theater," *Speculum*, 11 (1936), 171–211.

were deducing the use of secular, profane performing arts within the confines of the Byzantine liturgy, La Piana sure of only the sixth and seventh century dramatic homilies [*kontakia*] in this regard, Cottas much more receptive to them in a whole range of liturgical offices.

More recent writing on these questions appears to take the position of the earlier scholars for granted, while stressing the positive, creative adaptation of a secular and profane institution. I find little or nothing suggestive of the *contrafactum* in the discussions of such writers as Trypanis, Wellesz, Grosdidier de Matons, and Velimirovic. The dramatic homilies, especially those related to the Christmas liturgy, are seen as the products of a great original genius (Romanos the Melodist, primarily, but also of a school of highly gifted musical and poetic composers). From the experiments and imitations developed over a century and more of activity, the *kontakion* became a superb work of art, "the one and only great original achievement of Byzantine literature," as Trypanis puts it,[50] in "the golden age of Greek hymnography," as Tillyard designates it.[51]

The above sketch of the saint's vigil festivities in the East during the period of the fourth to seventh centuries may serve as background for the similar developments in southern Gaul, in the area now known as Provence. The principle of the *contrafactum* was operative here, but it encountered severe opposition from some ecclesiastical leaders, above all from Caesarius, Bishop of Arles in the early sixth century. Nevertheless, the spirit of the *contrafactum* was responsible for some highly creative strategies that ultimately transformed the saint's vigil, using the tradition of recitative from ancient Roman theatrical practice and refining it into a public narrative art. Thus the presentation

50. Trypanis, ed., *Sancti Romani Melodi Cantica Genuina* (Oxford: Clarendon Press, 1963), p. xiv. I am indebted to a graduate student of mine, now Dr. Alice Mandanis, for introducing me to the work of Romanos.

51. H. J. W. Tillyard, *Byzantine Music and Hymnography* (London: Faith Press, 1923, AMS Reprint, New York, 1976), p. 18.

of the saint's life became a paraliturgical event of great significance.

Provence was the last territory in the Western Empire to support a classical humanistic culture before the fall of Rome itself. It had possessed a continuous intellectual tradition for centuries, first as the site of a Greek colony in Marseilles and later as a bastion of Latin thought and literature against the advancing lines of successive barbarian invasions from the north. Refugees from devastated cities like Trier, and even from nearby Aquitaine, made their way into this corner of southeastern Gaul, in search of physical safety and also of letters and learning, still flourishing there.[52] The area itself eventually succumbed to the waves of barbarism, but it was able to preserve a flourishing literary culture through the fourth and fifth centuries and to maintain a philosophical ideal of balance and natural wisdom that it had inherited from the Graeco-Roman civilization of earlier centuries.

The classical humanism of Provence served as a deterrent not only to the invading tribal societies of the Visigothic people, but also to the Oriental movement of monasticism that flowed into southern Gaul during the same centuries. This is the position of Nora Chadwick; she sees the bishops of Gaul, learned and cultivated men, as challenged and uneasy over the temper of the new monastic asceticism. This movement seemed at first to be as thoroughly non-Roman in its Eastern asceticism as the lifestyle of the Visigothic invading armies, and in her view, the triumph of the Oriental alien force was made possible by the simultaneous impact of these two invasions. Roman Christian culture finally succumbed to the attraction of Eastern forms of spirituality because the Classicism of the Roman temperament had been weakened and overwhelmed by the Germanic onslaught.[53] This is a large and debatable historical outlook, and is

52. Nora Chadwick, *Poetry and Letters in Early Christian Gaul* (London: Bowes and Bowes, 1955), p. 160.
53. Ibid., pp. 60–61, 142, et passim.

complicated by the fact that many of the bishops in Gaul were actually educated in the new monastic centers during the fifth century, especially at Lérins, the island retreat close to Marseilles that was itself to become the leading intellectual center of the Western Mediterranean for a long period.

One is not constrained to accept the total view of Chadwick on the relationship of monasticism and the episcopacy in order to appreciate the role of Roman Classicism in the cultural life of this area. The period of the Visigothic invasions in Gaul and Spain was one of learned and cultivated bishops, many of them closely associated with rising monastic centers and drawing upon their spiritual, philosophical, and literary resources. Conditions varied from one diocese to another, from one type of personal leadership to another, but the era after the fall of Rome was one in which great civil administrators in the outlying sections of the Roman world were chosen and even drafted into bishoprics, wherein they became local bastions of a disappearing ancient civilization.[54] Out of this political and social context the pastoral programs and the liturgical rites of the Gallican era developed. The central feature of those programs was the use of the saints' lives as the vehicle of religious instruction and of cultural literacy. From Sidonius Apollinaris to Caesarius of Arles in Gaul, and even to Isidore and Braulio in seventh-century Spain, the weight of Roman civilization served both as resource and as challenge to these statesmen-bishops. It is important to note that this general program was one that the Roman See itself did not support. It was a provincial phenomenon, officially discredited in papal and conciliar decrees over a period of centuries, as historians of the liturgy have clearly documented.[55]

The background of this episcopal leadership was aristocratic,

54. Ibid., passim; C. E. Stevens, *Sidonius Apollinaris and his Age* (Oxford: Clarendon Press, 1933), pp. 115–17.

55. B. de Gaiffier, "La Lecture des Actes des martyrs dans la prière liturgique en occident," *Analecta Bollandiana*, 72 (1954), 134–66, esp. p. 143. See also H. G. Muller, pp. 544–75, esp. p. 549; Martène, *De Antiquis*, I, 367; Mabillon, *DLG*, Col. 12, 26, 2.

insofar as such a term can be used of Western European society in the pre-feudal stages of its history. The bishops who emerged or who were thrust into positions of power were generally wealthy provincial landowners and public officials, sometimes with close family ties to the political life of Rome itself. Sidonius Apollinaris, for example, was a prominent public official through much of the mid-fifth century and was married to the daughter of the Roman Emperor Avitus. In 469 he was suddenly elected bishop of Clermont, where he finished his days as a leading ecclesiastic.[56]

The culture of Provence and its adjacent areas, therefore, contains the paradigm for the paraliturgical enterprise in the West, involving a Roman mimic tradition and an officially established practice of reading saints' lives to a congregation. Each of these components needs a special consideration in light of the surviving evidence, and we can turn first to the question of a continuous tradition of Roman theatrical performance of a mimic type. This continuity is revealed in casual allusions and in condemnations made by ecclesiastical leaders in various parts of the Empire but especially in southern Gaul.

Salvian, author of the *De Gubernatione Dei*, fled from Trier to Marseilles in the early fifth century. He gives a vivid picture of the cultivated Gallo-Roman Christian pursued by the specter of barbaric violence, and yet the fury that pervades his analysis of the late Roman Empire is directed rather at his fellow-Christians than at pagans (either of the Germanic or Roman stock). His book, written about 450, contains a large section condemning the public recreation of his day throughout the declining Empire as the leading symptom of a moral decadence undermining the whole populace and making it fair play for invaders from the north. Book VI of this work singles out the theater and the circus for excoriation, although he indicates that he is limiting himself to these institutions of Roman culture because he has

56. Stevens, pp. 113ff.

not time to treat all the forms of public pleasure and recreation that he has observed.[57]

H. Reich judged that Salvian threw the weight of his condemnation against the mimic performances rather than stage plays.[58] In his discussions of the theater, however, Salvian seems to be referring to both the legitimate stage and the mimic repertory and he uses the word *ludus* in both the narrow sense of stage play and the broad sense of show or spectacle.[59] In VI, iii, 15 he lists several types of entertainers that provoke his disgust, horrified as he is by "lusoriis" (players), "petaminariis" (tumblers), and "pantomimis" (silent mimic performers).[60] As he observes the Empire crumbling around him he sees Christians scorning the churches and honoring the theaters, running to plays, reveling at the circuses: "Ad ludos protinus curritur . . . , in circis plebs tota bacchatur" (VI, xviii, 95); "nos ecclesiis dei ludicra anteponimus, nos altaria spernimus et theatra honoramus . . ." (VI, vii, 36). He thus gives testimony to the flourishing of both plays and mimes as living theatrical phenomena in the mid-fifth century.

There are allusions to mimic activity also in the writings of Sidonius Apollinaris (c. 431–c. 487). These references are striking for the much more relaxed way in which they are made. There is nothing of Salvian's impassioned denunciation of a Roman world that is laughing itself to death at scurrilous plays and mimes, as indeed there is nothing of Augustine's and Jerome's anxiety over the threat of pagan Roman literature and drama. Sidonius, a resident of Gaul, writes in his letters about Roman

57. *De Gubernatione Dei*, ed. Carolus Halm, *Monumenta Germaniae Historica*, (Berlin: Weidmann, 1877).

58. Reich says: "Auch gendenkt Salvianus . . . des Mimus als des grossen Theaterstückes," (*Der Mimus*, Berlin: Weidmann, 1903), p. 778.

59. Salvian, VI, vii, 36, and xvii–xviii.

60. O'Sullivan gives this equivalent for "petaminariis" in his translation of the section. (*The Writings of Salvian, the Presbyter*, tr. Jeremiah O'Sullivan [Washington: The Catholic University of America Press, 1962, Fathers of the Church, Vol. 3]).

theatrical activity as current in his day. His best-known allusion is to private dramatic reading rather than to performance, as he recounts his pleasure in reading Terence's *Hecyra* with his son and comparing it with a similar Greek play by Menander, the *Epitrepontes*.[61] He mentions the contemporary theater of Rome in two of his letters, in which the allusions seem to depict audience reactions rather than performance itself. In I, v, 10 he mentions being in Rome at the time of a wedding in the imperial family and of hearing everywhere, even in the theaters, the festive cry of "Thalassio" to the newlyweds. In I, x, 2 he expresses fear that a food shortage in Rome will be blamed on him as an incompetent public official and that the fury of the populace will find expression in the theaters. In one of his *Carmina* (XXIII, 263) he gives a detailed account of pantomimic performance at Narbonne (Mohr, pp. 344–45). In a letter to Agricola, son of the Emperor Avitus (*Ep.* I, ii) Sidonius speaks of mimes at the Visigothic court of Theodoric II in Gaul. Here he refers to the wit of the jesters ("mimici sales") and to the pleasing entertainment that Theodoric excluded from his meals, and the list serves to indicate what must have been common practice in the dining halls of the wealthy: playing of water-organs, choral singing and reading, lute performance, dance ensembles, and solo singing accompanied by the tambourine.

Quite different again from Sidonius' allusions are those of Caesarius, who became bishop of Arles after an education at the monastery of Lérins. In the life of this indefatigable man one can see the prodigious energy needed to administer a diocese in southern Gaul after the collapse of the Empire and the growth of a Christian population that was semiliterate. Nora Chadwick speaks of him as "one of the greatest men produced by the monastery of Lérins,"[62] and Max Laistner writes of him

---

61. C. Sollius Apollinaris Sidonius, ed. Paulus Mohr (Leipzig: Teubner, 1895), p. 87. No general title is given to this volume, which contains the letters and poems.

62. Chadwick, p. 185.

as primarily an effective preacher in an era when the clergy were not only spiritual leaders but also educators of their people, indeed the only instruments of formal education for most of them.[63] Caesarius is the most important single figure in the experiments that produced the Gallican liturgy of France and the related Hispanic liturgy of the Iberian peninsula.

In his younger years at Lérins, the island monastery off the southeast coast of France, Caesarius had missed the greatest days when this institution was a leading intellectual center of the West. Nevertheless, his education was good. The decline of enthusiasm for classical humanistic studies, particularly rhetoric, marked the whole generation at the turn of the sixth century. Caesarius' own attempt to study eloquence and his abrupt withdrawal from the endeavor must be understood against this "Spirit of the Age," a viewpoint notably dominant then at Lérins, and strengthened by the chaotic conditions of a public life that could no longer nourish scholarly leisure and cultivation of literary skills. Caesarius developed a general suspicion about secular learning in the Latin tradition, and failed to acquire a literary style that could have distinguished his large and impressive collection of sermons.[64]

Caesarius became openly hostile to the theatrical performances of his day, the tradition of Roman public entertainment, including the animal combats and the mimic repertory of recitation, music, and dance. He, of course, knew of Augustine's hostility before his time. In several of his sermons Caesarius severely denounces the *spectacula* (shows), and in these invectives gives testimony to the continued flourishing of the circus and the theater in the Gaul of his day. It is remarkable that he uses the same three adjectives whenever he condemns the *spectacula:* "cruenta," "turpia," and "furiosa." The term "cruenta"

63. M. L. W. Laistner, *Thought and Letters in Western Europe, 500–900,* rev. ed. (Ithaca, N.Y.: Cornell University Press, 1957), pp. 126–127.

64. A. Malnory, *Saint Césaire, Évêque d'Arles, 504–543* (Paris: Librairie Émile Bouillon, 1894, rpt. Geneva: Slatkine Reprints, 1978), pp. 18–20.

may still refer to gladiatorial combat, but probably means animal baiting; "turpia" indicates pornographic entertainment; "furiosa" is the most difficult to interpret, but probably means frenetic revelry and dance. His most general condemnation of these theatrical spectacles occurs in Sermon 150, in which he lists various types of sinners and thus specifies those who love the public shows: "spectacula vel cruenta vel furiosa vel turpia diligentes."[65] It is in Sermon 89 that he uses the most precise language, castigating one who chooses rather to frequent the public *spectacula* than to attend church and listen to the sacred reading ("cum deberet lectioni insistere . . . eligit potius . . . spectacula . . . frequentare.")[66] The opposition drawn here between attending the liturgical reading at church ("lectioni insistere") and attendance at the public *spectacula* is a strong indication that Caesarius regarded the ecclesiastical reading of lections (including saints' lives) as an antidote and substitute for the dangerous theatrical performances.

In a number of his sermons this ardent bishop explicitly condemns miming and dancing without referring to public shows in general. These references are clearly connected with the celebration of saints' festivals, that is, the annual feast days of various martyrs. In both Gaul and Spain these celebrations attracted groups of choral dancers and singers, who transferred to the sanctoral holy day the type of festivity that had formerly marked the ancient pagan cult of the gods. Condemnations of this practice by the Church councils of Toledo III and of Chalon make this fact absolutely certain.[67] As in the Byzantine territory,

65. Caesarius of Arles, *Sermones*, ed. Germain Morin, rev. ed., *Corpus Christianorum: Series Latina*, Vols. 103–4 (Turnhout, Belgium: Brepols, 1953), II, 615. In Sermon 12 he denounces these public demonstrations as the work of the devil (ibid., I, 61); in Sermon 134 he urges his listeners to reprove any of their fellow Christians who frequent the *spectacula*, and to pray earnestly for their repentance (ibid., I, 550).

66. Ibid., I, 368.

67. Third Council of Toledo, Canon 23, in J. D. Mansi, ed., *Sacrorum Conciliorum et Decretorum Nova et Amplissima Collectio* (Leipzig: Welter, 1901), Vol. 9, Col. 999 (589 A.D.); Council of Chalon, Canon 19, in *Concilia Galliae, A. 511–A.*

the devotion to the saints was encouraged by the Gallic bishops of France and Spain,[68] as a *contrafactum*, as a way of freeing the people from pagan superstitions and of teaching Christian holiness to them.[69] These festivals then became the focus of ancient practices that simply persisted in the dancing and singing groups, forcing the ecclesiastical leaders to condemn them, and prompting conciliar decrees against desecration of the saints' festivals.

This theme of condemnation runs through many of the sermons delivered by Caesarius and underscores his importance in the controversy. As the metropolitan bishop of Arles he had authority over some twenty-five or thirty bishops in his province, and general supervision over ecclesiastical matters in both Gaul and Spain, including church councils held there.[70] The language of his sermons emphasizes the various elements that belonged to traditional popular celebrations: dancing, pantomime, speech, and song, all of which he castigates as vile in content and pagan in origin. These elements constitute the Roman secular drama of the late Empire, and are traceable all through the history of Rome as part of the dramatic tradition. The words that Caesarius uses for dancing are *ballare*, *saltare*, and *choros ducere*, and for the singing *cantare* and *decantare*.[71] He is particularly outraged that these performances take place in

695, ed. Carolus de Clercq (Turnhout, Belgium: Brepols, 1963), Vol. 138A, p. 307, (Council held about 647–53). A similar prohibition was made by the Council of Auxerre in 573, but its Latin is difficult to interpret. (*Concilia Galliae*, loc. cit., p. 265).

68. H. G. J. Beck, *The Pastoral Care of Souls in South-East France during the Sixth Century* (Rome: Gregorian University, 1950), pp. 307–8; Caesarius of Arles, Sermons 223, 224, 225.

69. Hillgarth, p. 51; É. Mâle, *La Fin du paganisme en Gaule* (Paris: Flammarion, 1950), pp. 54–69; Pierre Salmon, ed., *Le Lectionnaire de Luxeuil*, IX, 65–66.

70. Caesarius, *Sermons*, tr. Sister M. M. Mueller (New York: Fathers of the Church, 1956–73), I, Introduction, ix–x.

71. Caesarius, *Sermons* 13, 16, 55, 216, 223, 225. R. Foatelli (p. 46) translates the phrase "Chorum ducere" as "Conduire des rondes dansantes," singling out the rhythmic movement rather than the language (in Durandus of Mende's *Rationale Divinorum Officiorum* allusion). *Les Danses religieuses dans la christianisme*, 2nd. ed. (Paris: Éditions Spes, 1947).

front of the very basilicas dedicated to the saints.[72] Moreover, he recognizes that participants in this revelry were often in a state of inebriation which itself desecrated the sanctoral feast day.[73] He clearly denounces the nature of the celebrations as pagan traditions, and tells his congregations that those who participated came to the church as Christians but returned home as pagans, because the custom was a survival from paganism: "Ista consuetudo ballandi de paganorum observatione remansit."[74]

These statements of official condemnation and sometimes of relaxed observation by Salvian, Sidonius, and Caesarius form a continuous thread of evidence for the Roman mimic tradition. This continuity was active and influential from the last years of the Empire until well into the seventh century, far into the era of the Gallic liturgies. It is capable of interpretation as threat or ally to Christian life, depending upon the personal viewpoint of the writer and the circumstantial context of a particular time and place, just as it had been in the East. Upon this tradition of professional performance I would superimpose the practice of the public recitation given to saints' lives during the hegemony of these liturgies in Gaul and Spain. This mode of public reading at Matins and Mass was a consciously structured experiment in religious education, undertaken as a rival attraction to the frequently scandalous repertory of the mimes and actually drawing upon the techniques of the secular theater. Thus the saint's *vita* emerges as an expression of the instinct for dramatic entertainment that E. K. Chambers recognized as endemic to the Western Mediterranean world. Instead of viewing the Christian clergy as enemies of that instinct for drama, as he did,[75] I say that by and large the clergy, under the patronage and leadership of great bishops like Caesarius, fostered the popular desire in a modified form, a *contrafactum*, by giving to their congregations

72. Sermon 13 (I, 67).   73. Sermons 16, 55, and 225.
74. Sermon 13.
75. Chambers, *The Mediaeval Stage*, I, Chapter I.

on major saints' festivals a form of public reading worthy of comparison with the repertory and skill of the *mimi*, and at times making use of the professional performers as the reciters and dancers themselves. This idea is the subject of the chapters to follow. Episcopal patronage, then, is the key to the cultural phenomenon. The bishops, contrary to Chambers' famous judgment, did not join the barbarians to destroy the ancient theater,[76] but rather to preserve it in a modified form of singular power.

76. Ibid., p. 22.

CHAPTER IV

THE RECITATION OF THE SAINT'S LIFE IN THE GALLICAN AND HISPANIC LITURGIES

The biography of a saint was one of the most popular forms of literature throughout the Middle Ages, when it often served as a major type of heroic, even flamboyant story-telling with incidents and characters akin to those of epic, *chanson de geste*, or courtly romance.[1] The saint's legend participated in the meaning and the literary style of these genres successively, according to the spirit of the age and the quality of cultural life in each particular era. In Western Europe, especially in France, the interrelation of hagiography with the early vernacular heroic narrative has long been a subject of historical interest, but a connection with dramatic tradition has not been recognized. Before the scholar can attempt to construct a connection of the saint's *vita* with theater, he needs to ponder the place of the legend in the liturgy of the medieval Church, and more precisely, of the Gallican and Hispanic rites. The fundamental source of historical knowledge on the subject is the work of Gregory of Tours, but this imposing record of civil and religious life in Gaul needs to be supplemented by a study of the surviving Latin sacramentaries and lectionaries used in Gallican churches of the sixth and immediately following centuries. Although Gregory's text has been mined by modern historians, beginning with Jean Mabil-

1. I have considered these literary relations in "The Saint's Legend as History and as Poetry: An Appeal to Chaucer," *American Benedictine Review,* 27 (1976), 357–77.

lon,[2] for its references to the liturgy, the net result of such inves-
tigation is a set of very casual allusions often pointed by Gregory toward some public event or a personality who happened
to be involved in a Mass celebration or a Matins office. These
references are precious by their incidental nature, revealing that
Gregory is taking them for granted as things widely known and
accepted. He is not engaged in an antiquarian's account of the
liturgy itself. Consequently, his information needs to be supplemented by the actual texts of the Mass and the Divine Office,
and it is the aim of this chapter to make such a supplementary
excursion into the Gallican books.

The public reading of a saint's life has never been favored by
those responsible for the Roman liturgy. Various reasons have
been deduced to account for this bias, and it seems to me that
all these reasons share in a basic judgment of the phenomenon
as *provincial*, in the full sense of that word. As I indicated in the
chapter on Mabillon, the Roman preoccupation with the universal scope and the heavy responsibilities of a central administra-
tion gives to its liturgy a grave and juridical cast that generally
discourages the popular expression of devotion and a popular
orientation of the liturgy.[3] Moreover, the real possibility that the
saint's life could become a vehicle of heresy made it suspect as
a form of lection in the Mass when it was substituted for Scriptural readings.[4] Here again, the concern with orthodoxy tends
to alienate the fringe phenomenon that has potential for uncon-
trolled growth and wild luxuriance. An aspect of the basic attitude may well be the sophistication of Roman devotional life,
founded on an ancient Mediterranean culture, classical in character and style. The extravagance of a provincial saint's life writ-

2. Gregory's text is edited in the *MGH* series: *Libri Historiarum X*, rev. ed., ed.
Bruno Krusch and W. Levison (Hannoverae: Impensis Bibliopoli Hahniani,
1951). See also A. Marignan, *Le Culte des saints sous les Mérovingiens;* and O. M.
Dalton, tr., *The History of the Franks*, Vol. 1 (commentary).

3. Leclercq, "Gallicane (Liturgie)," *DACL*, Vol. 6, Col. 480.

4. H. F. Muller, "Pre-History of the Medieval Drama," pp. 548–53.

ten and recited in Gaul amid the violence and turmoil of the Frankish rule might well seem barbaric to Roman taste. When the low level of Latin education in the Frankish kingdoms is considered in the context of linguistic decline in both spoken and written composition, the public recitation of a saint's life can be seen as a trivial, ignorant, and romantic expression, embarrassing to Rome and a scandal to the congregations themselves. It is worthy of note that many centuries later, when the Bollandist project of the Jesuits was presented to Cardinal Bellarmine for approval, the eminent ecclesiastic demurred and hesitated to encourage the printed publication of the *Acta Sanctorum* for exactly the same reason: he regarded many of the saints' *vitae* as romantic, popular compositions that would raise laughter in an educated seventeenth century French audience and create scandal rather than devotion.[5]

The enthusiasm for saints' lives in Gaul and Spain, on the other hand, seems to have been a natural growth of popular devotion among newly converted Christians, and an integral part of the local cultural heritage, outlasting even the reimposition of the Roman rite by the Council of 789 (Aix-la-Chapelle).[6] Marignan gives considerable weight to the tenacity of pagan customs in Gaul long after the acceptance of Christianity. He observes that celebration on the feasts of the ancient gods continued to find expression in popular life as a natural force in ethnic culture, and that this festive spirit found its external manifestation in song and dance.[7] Moreover, he adds, the newly received converts found the Christian liturgy a heavy burden incomprehensible to them, for it required a disciplined attention to clerical chanting for long periods in the Divine Office and in the Mass. Restive at this genuine difficulty, they

5. Dunn, "The Saint's Legend as History," p. 359.
6. The Ambrosian rite of Milan is a more obscure case, but saints' lives were a prominent feature of it for some centuries.
7. Marignan, p. xiii.

tended to fall into private conversation during the services or to leave after the lections had been read to them, sometimes missing the essential part of the Mass.[8]

Dom Pierre Salmon, in a study of a Gallican service book, has written that paganism retained its hold on the people in much of Gaul, especially in the rural areas. Christianity found acceptance in the cities, where many churches were built and maintained, but the countryside remained largely pagan throughout the Gallican era. Temples of the ancient gods continued in use, and actual beliefs and customs survived. Repeated waves of Germanic invasion reinforced the grass-roots culture of this type, especially in the northeastern part of the country, and the rustic population often reverted to paganism even if it had once accepted Christianity.[9] The education of the clergy in these rural areas was poor and the level of their spirituality mediocre. Inevitably, then, the religious life of Christian parishes was immature, even primitive, and the tenacity of ancient folk ways is surely not a matter for surprise. With an anachronistic background of this type, the spiritual culture even of the cities takes on a cast of instability and provincialism. Raymond Van Dam's recent study goes much further than Salmon, and presents the church of Gaul as much like a church independent of the Roman see.[10]

A. Marignan indicates that since the traditional pagan festivals continued to be marked by age-old rejoicing and ceremonial, local ecclesiastical authorities took two measures of dealing with this recalcitrance. One was to inveigh against it in conciliar decrees, as in the Council of Chalon, c. 639,[11] which explicitly

8. Mabillon, *DLG*, loc. cit., Col. 126, 27–28, 4. See Sermons 73 and 74 of Caesarius.

9. Salmon, *Le Lectionnaire de Luxeuil*, 9 [1953], 65–66.

10. Ibid., p. 77; Van Dam, *Leadership and Community in Late Antique Gaul*, pp. 166–83. Van Dam gives a detailed picture of the family of Gregory of Tours as worldly and politically manipulative (pp. 205–13), but scarcely mentions Caesarius of Arles, whose episcopal leadership was energetic, zealous, and orthodox.

11. Marignan, p. xiv n. 1. I consider this canon of the Council in another chapter (V).

mentioned church dedications and the festivals of martyrs as occasions that had been abused by these practices. The second disciplinary measure, and one that marks the general policy of the Church throughout the early Middle Ages in similar problems, was to adapt the pagan festival by giving it a new meaning, leaving much of the external activity intact in a wise toleration of popular exuberance.[12] In this way the festival of a Christian saint would become the focus of the ancient folk activities, so that song and dance would mark the popular expression of hagiographical devotion. The celebration would parallel and supplement the more formal liturgy performed by the clergy inside the churches. This was an early manifestation of the paraliturgical implementation that the Latin liturgy, in its gravity and sublimity, frequently needed and has been given from time to time,[13] for example, in the musical troping of the Carolingian era, and in the vernacular mystery cycles of the late Middle Ages.

The particular phase of the festivity which came to mark the saint's day in the Gallican era was the public reading of a martyr's or a confessor's life story. Salmon indicates that the custom has Spanish origins, but Mabillon, in his pioneer study, had not recognized an indebtedness of Gaul to Spain in the matter.[14] Whatever may be the origin and age of the practice,[15] there are

12. É. Mâle discusses the long process of countering the persistence of pagan religions. Sometimes the pagan temples were destroyed, especially in the evangelization achieved by St. Martin in the fourth century (pp. 32–37). Often a Christian chapel or church was built on a spot sacred to Celtic worship of lakes, forests, mountains, and streams (pp. 54–69).

13. Karl Rahner, *The Christian Commitment: Essays in Pastoral Theology,* tr. Cecily Hastings (New York: Sheed and Ward, 1963), pp. 174–75, notes this perennial need.

14. Salmon, *Le Lectionnaire,* 7 (1944), pp. lxxvi and lxxviii. (The two volumes of Salmon's work appeared years apart.)

15. G. R. Coffman has said that the earliest record of martyrs' lives forming lections of the Divine Office occurs in Aurelian of Arles' *Regula ad Monachos,* a sixth-century monastic rule. (*A New Theory,* p. 35). B. de Gaiffier, "La Lecture des actes des martyrs," discusses the Spanish records on pp. 153–56 and somewhat hesitantly gives the seventh century as affording the earliest documented testimony for Spain. See below, n. 24.

remote analogues for the custom of honoring a saint in such a public way. Augustine, in *De Civitate Dei*, recounts the miracles attributed to St. Stephen, whose relics had been enshrined in some North African churches. When a cure occurred after prayers to Stephen, the person so affected would be asked to compose a written account of the miracle in the form of a *libellus*, an official deposition, which would then be recited to an assembled congregation in praise of God and His holy one. Such a practice provided a kind of tradition for the public honoring of a saint in later eras.[16]

Contemporary with Augustine's encouragement of devotion to St. Stephen was the cultivation of popular piety toward St. Felix by Paulinus of Nola in Campania. Although the shrine of Felix was located in Italy, Paulinus was himself a native of southern Gaul, a wealthy landowner born in Bordeaux in 353. He had been governor of Campania, in which Nola was located, and after a retirement from public life and a spectacular conversion to a kind of monastic spirituality,[17] he drew great crowds of pilgrims to Felix's shrine and composed an anniversary poem (*natalicium*) to be read to the people each year, two of which poems (Nos. 15 and 16) are a *vita* of the saint.[18] Many of Paulinus' audience were simple peasants, but he drew upon his own classical education as the beloved student of the poet Ausonius, and interlaced his tributes to Felix with allusions to Vergil's poetry, which have been carefully annotated by his modern translator.[19] Paulinus' endeavor is a good illustration of the *contrafactum* in operation, as the anniversary poem was an imitation of the classical genre known as the *genethliakon*. Although the classical context must have been lost on the rustic members of his con-

---

16. *De Civitate Dei*, Bk. 22, viii, 10–22. For an account of Augustine's practice, see Fray Justo Perez de Urbel's edition of the *Liber Commicus*, a medieval lectionary, incorporating these miracles, I, lxxxvi.

17. Nora Chadwick, pp. 70–84.

18. Paulinus, *Carmina*, ed. Guilelmus de Hartel (Vienna: *CSEL*, 1894), 30.

19. *The Poems of St. Paulinus of Nola*, trans. and annotated P. G. Walsh (New York: Newman Press, 1975).

gregation, Paulinus knew that he had at least a small audience of highly cultivated readers in Aquitaine, to whom he sent the poems, notably Sulpicius Severus, himself the biographer of St. Martin.[20] The *natalicia* are sprinkled with casual allusions to the splendor of the ceremony that Paulinus held, and to the cosmopolitan crowds that flocked on pilgrimage to Nola.[21]

Peter Brown has a fine passage in which he gives Paulinus a place beside Augustine in the development of Christian spirituality.[22] There are two aspects to his religious life, first, this popular cult of a saint, and second, his role in the development of Western monasticism. Although the latter work is outside the scope of the present study, it is an important element in the context of hagiographical devotion in the centuries leading up to the Gallican era. F. J. Raby viewed him as "deeply moved by the religious revival which, under the influence of Martin of Tours, was then sweeping over the south of Gaul."[23] Even though the documentation for the public reading of saints' lives belongs to the centuries following the fall of Rome, the Gallican practice has an underlying affinity with these earlier currents of Christian life that should not easily be dismissed as superstitions or as merely provincial.[24]

In the Gallican service books that have survived and been edited in modern times, the public memorial of a saint's *vita* permeates the whole liturgy of the day, but especially in two places. The first occurs in the prayer that corresponds to the "Preface"

20. Walsh, p. 12, p. 354 n. 49; p. 372 n. 5. See No. 16, 1.17 of the *Carmina* (Hartel's numbering) and Letter 28,6 in Paulinus' *Epistulae* (Vol. 29 of the *CSEL* series, also edited by Hartel).

21. See Nos. 18–29 of the *Natalicia,* following the *vita* of Felix.

22. Brown, *The Cult of the Saints*, pp. 53–55.

23. F. J. Raby, *Christian Latin Poetry,* 2d ed. (Oxford: Clarendon Press, 1953), p. 101. See also pp. 102–7; and Joseph Lienhard, S. J., *Paulinus of Nola and Early Western Monasticism* (Cologne–Bonn: Hanstein, 1977).

24. There are scattered references in early sermons of Gaul to the public reading of saints' lives in the fifth century, but their date is questionable. É. Griffe credits these allusions, with some hesitation, but B. de Gaiffier challenges him and insists on the sixth century as the earliest for the practice. (Griffe, *La Gaule chrétienne,* III, 216; de Gaiffier, "Aux Origines de la liturgie gallicane," p. 34).

of the Roman Mass, and, like the Preface, leads immediately into the "Sanctus." The second method is the more detailed account of the whole life placed as a lection in the solemn Matins office and at times continued in the day's Mass. Mabillon had knowledge of both types, but did not write an analysis of the texts in the service books he had discovered and studied.

Let us, therefore, consider these two methods of sanctoral veneration more closely. The first is a prayer in which a saint's marvellous acts would simply be summarized. This prayer in the Gallican rite is called the "Contestatio," and sometimes the "Immolatio." Corresponding to the Roman "Preface," it extols the majesty and power of God the Father. H. Leclercq has remarked that although the "Contestatio" begins with the formula for the Roman Preface, "Vere dignum et justum est," it is quite different in both content and style from the Preface, affording the modern reader an experience with a very strange Latin idiom combining solemn articulations of Christian doctrine and a mode of address stylized for an untutored and unlettered congregation.[25] The "Contestatio" is markedly "proper" to the day's feast. On the saint's festival it could be a small-scale biography, drawing upon the more lengthy form of the *vita* available in a legendary. The saints who are notable for this manner of treatment in the Gallican books are John the Baptist, Peter, Andrew, Stephen, Leodgarius (Leger), Eulalia, Germain d'Auxerre, Remigius, Sigismund, Martin, and the monk St. Abraham. Leodgar and Eulalia take on a special interest because they are subjects of the earliest extant *vernacular* saints' lives in Old French.[26]

The miracles of St. Remigius, for example, have survived in a "contestatio" printed by Mabillon and edited among minor Gal-

25. Leclercq, "Preface," *DACL*, Vol. 14, Cols. 1713–14.
26. These two Latin *vitae* appear in the *Missale Gothicum,* ed. Cunibert Mohlberg.

lican texts in 1958 by Mohlberg.[27] Although it is a fragment, the prayer is quite lengthy, covering in its thirty-seven lines several miracles attributed to Remigius in a striking and charming account. Portrayed as a wonder-worker who resembles the Francis of Assisi yet to come in a later era, he emerges as one with special power over natural forces. He feeds thousands of wild sparrows from his hand, and as they flock tamely to him he draws upon a supply of crumbs and table food that remains miraculously undepleted.[28] When a great crowd of people is gathered before him and is suffering from thirst, Remigius prays for Divine assistance, and is given a large bowl from which the royal family and the whole gathering of people drink without diminishing the abundantly flowing liquid (apparently water). When he prepares to baptize a sick person, and finds that no chrism is available, he places empty vessels on the altar table, into which a heavenly dew of the holy oil gathers at his prayer.[29]

A second saint who figures prominently in the "contestatio" is St. Germain d'Auxerre. The first Mass in the *Missale Gallicanum Vetus* is dedicated to this bishop of Auxerre and famous preacher of the Gospel in France, Italy, and England, according to the account. The prayer opens with an expression of thanksgiving addressed to God the Father, and then moves into a generalized presentation of Germain's sanctity revealed in his contempt of worldly wealth, his gentleness, his hunger and thirst for justice, his almsgiving and purity of heart. The catalogue of virtues is clearly adapted from the evangelical Beatitudes, but the account becomes more personalized as his apostolic work is added to his interior dispositions.[30] He is spoken of as combat-

---

27. *Missale Gallicanum Vetus*, ed. Cunibert Mohlberg (Rome: Herder, 1958). The Remigius fragment is part of an Appendix in this edition, pp. 91–92. Mabillon had included it as an appendix to his *Annales Ordinis S. Benedicti* (Paris, 1703).

28. *Missale G. V.*, p. 92.

29. Ibid.

30. This text is regarded as a sacramentary of the Auxerre diocese. The account of the saint's virtues occurs on p. 4.

ting heresy, healing the sick, restoring the dead to life, and developing the life of faith in people to whom he preached in many locales.[31] Written in a Latin that is becoming primitive Romance, the text is almost illegible because of its orthography and its falling inflections,[32] but it reveals an effective fusion of Gospel content with saint's legend. A comparable life of St. Germain appears among the so-called "Mone Masses," a small book containing Gallican Sunday Masses and a special one for the feast of St. Germain.[33] This "contestatio" lists the virtues and achievements of St. Germain, but it is clearly not the same text as that of the *Missale Gallicanum Vetus*.[34] Both versions, however, emphasize the personal holiness of the man rather than the aggregation of miracles wrought through his intercession.

The Hispanic or Mozarabic rite contains a prayer corresponding to the Gallican "contestatio" and named the "inlatio." This address to the Father resembles the Gallican rather than the Roman Preface in its length and in the occasional use of the prayer for surveying a saint's life. A good example of the Spanish model can be found in the "inlatio" for the feast of St. Clement, covering two columns of the folio-sized page in the *Liber Mozarabicus Sacramentorum*.[35] One of the miracles performed by him resembles that of Moses striking water from the desert rock. The little *vita* tells that Clement brought forth gushing water from a

31. Ibid., pp. 4–5.

32. A useful survey of the inflectional and orthographic peculiarities of the Latin language in the sixth–seventh centuries can be found in P. Salmon's edition of the *Luxeuil Lectionary*, Vol. 7, Introduction. Mabillon's edition of the *Missale G. V.* normalizes the spelling in classical form.

33. They are designated by the name of Franz Joseph Mone, a nineteenth-century German scholar who discovered and first edited them in 1850. See above, Ch. II, n. 5. Neale and Forbes call this book the *Missale Richenovense*, regarding it as a possession of the Abbey of Reichenau. (*The Ancient Liturgies of the Gallican Church*), p. vi.

34. One can easily compare it with the latter, in Mohlberg's edition of the Mone Masses as an appendix to the *Missale G. V.*, pp. 89–91.

35. *Monumenta Ecclesiae Liturgica*, ed. Dom Marius Férotin, Vol. VI, cols. 39–41.

hidden vein in the earth revealed to him by a miraculous sign. Instead of using a rod, in the manner of Moses, Clement set up a tree branch in the earth at the spot of the hidden stream.[36]

The "inlatio" for St. Martin's feast day is a prayer of comparable length with St. Clement's. In addition to the catalogue of the virtues and miracles, it has a lyrical quality of exultation and eulogy different not only from the Roman Preface but also from the usual Gallican "contestatio," both of which have a greater sobriety of rhetoric. At one point the basic voice in the prayer addresses Martin: "O beatum uirum naturam saeculi respuentem, qui per diuersos generose anime motus, diuersos meruit habere triumphos! Insignis mundi contemptor, et eximia nostri seculi gloria: maior semper merito quam iudicio, Angelorum comes, consors Apostolice dignitatis."[37]

While the Gallican "contestatio" and the Hispanic "inlatio" were one way of expressing intense and fervent devotion to the saint in the authorized liturgies of these territories, the second method of veneration was more festive. It was the public reading of a full-scale *vita* in the Matins Office and in the Mass. This kind of honor paid to the spiritual hero has the character of a performance, a kind of folk celebration freely associated with the liturgy but detachable from it. It may well be related to pagan *dramatic* customs rather than to Christian practice. The fragmentary and scattered testimony to this popular mode of rejoicing suggests a limitation of it to very few saints' festivals and to a role that was extraordinary and paraliturgical rather than a regular feature of the public prayer life. Moreover, the practice

---

36. Ibid., Col. 40.
37. Ibid., Col. 398, ll. 27–32. (O blessed man spurning the world, who through the various affections of a noble soul merited to achieve many different victories! Eminent despiser of the world and distinguished glory of our age: always greater in kindness than in condemnation, companion of the angels and sharer in Apostolic dignity.) One of the Medieval Latin orthographic features in the passage is the spelling of Classical "ae" as "e," for example, in the feminine genitive singular.

seems to have been a diocesan one, a "secular" as opposed to a monastic church activity, and in this way different from the monastic liturgical Easter plays of the later Carolingian era.

The saint's life was read often in solemn Matins. The only modern scholar who has emphasized the significance of this fact, as far as I know, is Dom Pierre Salmon. As mentioned previously, solemn Matins was an especially elaborate and lengthy celebration of a major feast like Christmas or Easter, and belonged to the evening before the great day, thus anticipating the dawn by many hours and constituting a night office in the full sense of the word.[38] In the solemn form of the evening service, the presence of the laity was expected, and is more easily comprehensible than it would be in the early hours before dawn. I am convinced that many quotations from historical studies of this period need to be reinterpreted in terms of the word "vigiliae," which has often been mistranslated as the *day* of anticipation instead of as the solemn Matins office.

The extant Gallican service books for the Canonical Hours are few and some of them are incomplete. They make any generalizations about their contents and the related practices very difficult. The only general practice in the recitation of the Divine Office that Salmon regards as fully documented is the one of which we are now speaking: the reading of the lives of martyrs at solemn Matins. "Seule, peut-être," he writes, "la lecture des *gesta martyrum* aux vigiles est-elle assez attestée pour que l'on puisse la considérer comme une pratique générale."[39] He adds that the saint's life included in the Mass lections would usually have been started in the solemn night office of the previous evening's *vigiliae* and been simply continued in the Mass until the completion of the story.[40]

---

38. Salmon, IX, 60–61 and n. 98. Mabillon makes the same distinction between "Vigiliae" and "Matutinae," and says that "Vigiliae" began at least by midnight (*De Cursu Gallicano*, Col. 405, Sect. 421).

39. Salmon, IX, 57.

40. Ibid., IX, 59–60.

Since the Gallican feasts of saints are very few, and the same ones do not appear throughout the surviving lectionaries and missals, the rarity of sanctoral feasts should be regarded as a Gallican characteristic, and it reveals the great age of the sources upon which these liturgical books drew.[41] The Luxeuil Lectionary has only ten sanctoral feasts: Stephen, John the Evangelist, Holy Innocents, Genevieve, the Virgin Mary, Chair of Peter, John the Baptist, Peter and Paul, the *Passio* of John the Baptist, and Sts. Julian and Basilissa.[42]

The rarity of the saint's festival and the solemnity of its celebration encourage the judgment that it was special in every way, not an ordinary and regular occurrence.[43] It was associated with pilgrimage shrines and extraordinary occasions of celebration, perhaps occurring only once or twice a year at any particular locale. This very limitation of the practice in place and time produced the context in which a recitation of the saint's life could be a professional activity, a performing art, rather than a normal clerical chanting of the Divine Office. Those who were equipped for this kind of public entertainment were not the Gallican clergy but the professional *mimi* or *joculatores,* whose role must be given special consideration.

Marignan's description of the Gallican saint's festival rests solidly on a pilgrimage basis, which he typifies as a sixth-century occurrence representative of the Gallican era. He says that a bishop would most probably offer the Mass at a popular shrine, and where the ordinary reading of the three lections would have taken place (prophetic, epistolary, evangelical), the saint's life would be substituted as lectionary material. The moment was a solemn and awesome one, in which the lector would unfurl the scroll volume, announce the name of the saintly hero,

41. Ibid., VII, xci and IX, 48–51.
42. Ibid., IX, chart opposite p. 49.
43. Ibid., VII, lxxxviii. Salmon observes that it is difficult to say how extensive the custom of reading the martyr's *passio* in the Mass really was, and "il est fort possible qu'il ait été très restreint."

and begin his story. In the tense silence that only a fascinating narrative could create in this restless audience, the great heroic deeds would emerge. Frequently, Marignan adds, miracles of healing occurred right there during the recitation, as the sick who had come experienced the fulfillment of the devotion they had practiced in the name of the holy intercessor.[44]

Gregory of Tours records two miracles that occurred during the public reading of St. Martin's life. In the first one, two blind men, their eyelids congealed, prayed at the shrine while the saint's *vita* was being read. Suddenly a brilliant flash of light broke upon the crowd and the two men experienced a rupture of their sealed lids, a flow of blood from the eyes, and a completely restored vision.[45] The second miracle took place also on Martin's feast day, while crowds of pilgrims were gathered at his tomb, among them a man with a crippled arm. He is pictured as kissing the tomb and moistening it with his tears, trusting that he would eventually be healed through Martin's intercession. As the appointed lector began to read the life, the man immediately stood up, extended his arm straight, and proclaimed that his long-continued prayers had finally been answered with a perfect cure.[46] Martin of Tours is known as one of the most popular saints of all times and his tomb was a focal point for countless pilgrims and many miracles.[47]

A well-known passage of Gregory's *In Gloria Martyrum* narrates a rather bizarre miracle on the day of St. Polycarp. "Lecta igitur passione cum reliquis lectionibus, quas canon sacerdotalis invexit tempus ad sacrificium offerendum advenit." The Mass having advanced beyond the reading of Polycarp's passion, then, preparation was being made for the Consecration. A deacon who was carrying the receptacle containing the sacred wa-

44. Marignan, *Le Culte des saints*, pp. 121–22.
45. Gregory, "De Virtutibus Martini Episcopi," Bk. II, Ch. 29, in *Miracula et Opera Minora*, Vol. I, Part 2, pp. 169–70.
46. Ibid., Ch. 49, p. 176.
47. The *Saint Andrew Daily Missal*, ed. Gaspar Lefebvre (Bruges: Abbey of St. André, 1956), p. 1627.

fers to the altar dropped it and was unable to reach his hand to lift the ciborium from the floor. As Gregory tells the story, the paralysis of the deacon's arm was a Divine revelation of a secret guilt on his part.[48]

The presence of the bishop, noted by Marignan, would not be simply an indication of the festival's solemnity in an honorary sense. It is the precise evidence that the splendid celebration of the saint's day belonged to the secular rather than to the monastic liturgy. Although G. R. Coffman cites Aurelian of Arles' *Regula* (sixth century) as the earliest testimony to the reading of a martyr's passion in the Divine Office (see n. 15), the custom does not appear to have been of major importance in monastic practice. The very passage to which he refers occurs in an appendix to Aurelian's monastic rule, as a two-sentence prescription: "In martyrum festivitatibus tres aut quatuor missae fiant. ["Missae" means here lections.] Primam missam de Evangelio legite, reliquas de passionibus martyrum."[49] This admonition occurs in provisions for the night office. Ferreolus of Uzès, author of another monastic rule, decreed that the deeds of martyrs, gathered and arranged for reading, should be recounted in the chapel for the community to hear. This short chapter of Ferreolus' *Regula* shows more concern for the diligent use of the monastic day than for a splendid performance comparable to those of the pilgrimage shrines.[50] Mabillon, in noting that Ferreolus and Aurelian prescribed the reading of saints' lives in their monastic rules, commented that the practice had

48. Gregory, *MGH, Miracula,* Vol. I, Pt. 2, pp. 95–96 (rpt., 1969). Salmon interprets the reference as made to Tierce in this passage, the hour preceding celebration of Mass. (IX, 59–60.)

49. Aurelian, *Regula ad Monachos,* ed. J. Migne, *PL,* Vol. 68, Col. 396. The word "missa" clearly means lection here, as it does in the *Liber Commicus,* where the "Oficio de San Gines" has a life of the saint entitled "Missa." (Op. cit., II, 736–38.)

50. Ferreolus, *Regula ad Monachos,* ed. J. Migne, *PL,* Vol. 66, (1859), Col. 965. Ferreolus wished that the saint's day should be observed not in a holiday spirit but in regular devotion, so that the community would offer praise to the martyr whose constancy in suffering had rendered the person distinguished and renowned.

been approved by the third Council of Carthage and that this custom was observed in "Viennensi et Arelatensi Ecclesiis,"[51] the word "Ecclesiis" referring to the diocesan churches of Vienne and Arles rather than to monastic chapels, in my judgment.

The Luxeuil Lectionary gives testimony to the reading custom as a secular observance. This text, the most important surviving Gallican liturgical book with evidence of sanctoral lections, is now regarded not as monastic but as the book commissioned by the cathedral church of Langres, an episcopal see near Luxeuil. Salmon considers it probable that the manuscript was copied for the cathedral church by monks working in the scriptorium of the nearby Luxeuil abbey.[52] He adds the general observation that Gallican service books are not likely to be monastic usages, although they might be copied for a secular church by monastic scribes. More and more the monasteries came to adopt the Benedictine Rule and to use the Roman liturgy, long before the metropolitan sees accepted this rite; and by the ninth century, he says, all monasteries in the Gallican territory were Benedictine.[53]

In summary, then, the context for the reading of a saint's legend to an assembled congregation is that of solemn Matins and Mass at a pilgrimage shrine gathering, performed according to the Gallican customs of a diocesan liturgy, for a popular audience rather than a religious community.

The surviving service books in the Gallican and closely related rites contain a few examples of the saint's life as a *genre,* placed in the Matins office and also in the Mass of the festal day. We can gain some knowledge of their tenor and general stylistics, but need to recognize that they were likely to be recorded rather in a separate book, a *passionarium* (for martyrs) or a *legen-*

51. *De Cursu Gallicano,* Cols. 396–98. This section of Mabillon's treatise deals with the recitation of the Divine Office in the general area of Marseilles.
52. *Le Lectionnaire de Luxeuil,* IX, 74–76.
53. Ibid., pp. 70–71 and 76–77.

darium (for confessors), as previously indicated. The texts that do survive are in Latin, often a Latin idiom that is alien to Classical style and close to a Romance language structure and vocabulary. The small number of the versions in lectionaries points to the pastoral use of saints' lives already existing in anthologies of sanctoral material or in the repertories of jongleuristic entertainers. The Gallican *lectionarium*, and the Spanish *liber commicus* that corresponds to it, normally contain only the three lections from the Old Testament, New Testament epistles, and Gospels, with the occasional presence of a saint's *vita* that would be substituted for one or both of the prophetic and Apostolic readings.

When a hagiographical lection does occur, it appears not to have been specially composed for the occasion itself but rather culled from the historical and biographical literature available in the area. Thus a uniform stylistic tradition discernible as a "lectionary style" within the liturgical texts cannot easily be established and verified. In the Luxeuil Lectionary the two saints' lives are those of Julian and Basilissa and the *passio* of Sts. Peter and Paul. The style of these narratives is slow and leisurely, with large elements of debate and controversy. Both of these narratives are of Eastern origin, with intricate paths of transmission to the West that have long puzzled historians.[54] In the Hispanic lectionary known as the *liber commicus*, the miracles of Saint Stephen in the Silos manuscript are drawn from Augustine's *City of God*, Book XXII;[55] the narrative of St. Helen's finding of the Cross is extracted from Eusebius' *Historia Ecclesiastica*;[56] the life of St. Martin is that written in the fourth century by

54. Salmon, VII, x and lxxvi, indicates that the entry of Eastern texts of this kind into Gaul is by way of the Spanish liturgy and more remotely from African sources.

55. *Liber Commicus*, ed. Fray Justo Perez de Urbel, I, 25–30.

56. According to Fray Justo, I, lxxxi, this lection appears in the manuscript *Liber Commicus* of León, still located in its original place, the cathedral of León, as Codex 2. He devotes Chapter IV of his Introduction to the description and history of this manuscript, but he does not include the Eusebius extract in his critical edition.

Sulpicius Severus;[57] a Marian lection at Silos for the Assumption (a late addition to the Spanish calendar of feasts) is a long extract from San Ildefonso's *De Virginitate Beatae Mariae;*[58] another Marian lection for this feast is entitled "La dormición y translación de la Virgen," in Fray Justo de Urbel's phrase.[59] Let us examine the lections in the Luxeuil text.

The feast of Sts. Julian and Basilissa in this lectionary coincided with that of the Epiphany (January 6) and was celebrated within the week of that greater feast. The story of their life and death is a lengthy one (thirty printed pages in Dom Salmon's edition).[60] The narrative resembles that of St. Cecilia's life, as Julian marries Basilissa only after a message from heaven assures him that his vocation to celibacy will be fulfilled. The Egyptian couple agree not to consummate the marriage, and they found a monastery for men and a convent for women in Antioch. The manuscript is defective in the account of Basilissa's

57. Ibid., I, cxxv. This lection appears in a manuscript codex of Santo Domingo de Silos (Arch. Mon 5), dated 1069. It is a special supplementary lectionary for three feasts added late to the Spanish liturgy: St. Martin, St. Michael, and the Assumption of Mary. A microfilm of the manuscript is in the Hill Monastic Library at Collegeville, Minnesota, numbered 33,688. I have read the *vita* in the modern edition of it by C. Halm in the CSEL series (*Sulpicii Severi Opera,* Vol. I [Vindobonae: apud C. Geroldi Filium, 1966]). Halm appears not to have used the Silos manuscript in his collation. According to information provided to me by Jonathan Black of the Hill Library, the Silos text has a series of Matins lections for St. Martin's feast day, divided into twenty-six chapters. It is an especially interesting example of a text not originally composed for the liturgical office itself, as it was written in the fourth century but included late in a Spanish lectionary.

58. This treatise, also contained in the Silos manuscript Arch. Mon. 5, is edited by Vicente B. Garcia as *La Virginidad perpetua de Santa Maria* (Santos Padres Españoles [Madrid: Biblioteca de Autores Cristianos, 1971], Vol. I. The Silos manuscript was used among others by Garcia, who dates it 1059 instead of 1069.

59. Fray Justo, pp. cxxv–cxxvi; this lection appears in a manuscript *Rituale Antiquissimum* of Silos dated 1039. It is Arch. Mon. 3 (Hill Library 33, 684; see Gamber, No. 392). This narrative of Mary's Assumption is available in Férotin's reprint of it, which I used, in *Monumenta Ecclesiae Liturgica,* VI, 786–95.

60. Salmon has not made a critical edition of the *Passio,* but gives the text as it appears in the Lectionary. He indicates the general relationships of the surviving manuscripts without attempting a *stemma codicum,* and refers the reader to the complete text in the Bollandist *Acta Sanctorum* for January (I, 575ff.). (Salmon, VII, lxxv–vi.)

death, but the persecution and martyrdom of Julian are given at length. He is apprehended by Marcianus, prefect of Antioch under Diocletian and Maximian, and witnesses the execution by fire of all his associates. Marcianus reserves punishment of Julian, hoping to win him over to paganism by kindly treatment. The story then becomes really the *vita* of Celsius, the young son of the prefect, who embraces Christianity in the light of Julian's steadfast adherence to it. Celsius brings about the conversion of his mother, but Marcianus remains obdurate and demands that his son and Julian offer sacrifice to the gods in the temple. In an incident that resembles the Biblical story of Samson, the statues of the gods and the temple itself are brought down at Julian's prayer and swallowed up in the earth. After a final confrontation Marcianus has both Christians put to death by the sword.[61]

The account of these trials and deaths is almost wholly in dialogue form. It abounds in long prayers addressed to God by Julian or one of his companions, and long argumentative speeches of questioning and defiance by Marcianus, Julian, and Celsius. Often the only narratory link of these tirades is a brief statement like "Sanctus Julianus dixit. . . . Haec audiens mulier, dixit" (p. 50), or "Marcianus praesis dixit" (p. 49). This style of discourse would have been eminently suited to choral reading, with a separate voice for each of the major characters and a basic voice for the narrator, as in the Gospel Passion of Christ chanted during Holy Week.[62] There is, however, no musical notation in the text, and no indication of anything more than a single lector's recitative.

61. Salmon, VII, xcv, notes that two fifteenth-century breviaries contain this feast of Julian and Basilissa, with Matins lectionary materials. One of them gives simply the *incipit* of the same *passio* that is present in the Luxeuil lectionary; the other breviary contains a complete Matins office with nine lections.

62. This is a thorny historical problem. Karl Young, *Drama of the Medieval Church*, I, 100–101 and 550–51, refused to accept the dramatic chanting of the Passion in Holy Week, with impersonation of individual characters, as attested by manuscripts earlier than the fifteenth century. However, French scholars have been much more amenable to the acceptance of early medieval occurrence (*melopée multiple*, as they call it). P. Salmon says, rather cautiously, of Gallican

The apocryphal *Passio Petri et Pauli* is the other legend appearing in the Luxeuil lectionary. (Dom Salmon does not reproduce the text, but refers the reader to the edition of the *passio* by Richard Adelbert Lipsius in 1891.[63] Salmon himself supplies a corpus of variant readings from the Luxeuil manuscript, which he has collated against the Lipsius text.[64]) The version of the legend here is the so-called "Marcellus-text," which takes its name from the son of a Roman city-prefect credited with the authorship of the story.[65] Marcellus was reputed to be a follower of Simon Magus (the Samaritan sorcerer of *Acts* 8:9–24). Both had listened to the preaching of Peter and had become his disciples, so that the *passio* features the rivalry of the sorcerer with the miraculous powers of Peter. Greek and Latin versions of this legend were widespread in the Middle Ages, both in independent texts and in collections of legends about the Apostles, a Latin version, for example, appearing in Ordericus Vitalis' *Historia Ecclesiastica.*[66]

In the persecution and martyrdom of Peter and Paul at Rome, the narrative thread is picked up at the arrival of Paul in Rome ("Cum uenisset Paulus Romam"),[67] where he is immediately confronted by Jewish zealots who denounce Peter to him for overturning traditional Judaic law, particularly on circumcision. Paul consents to a public debate of the issues, and promises

---

Holy Week: "Il semble cependant que la lecture de la Passion, combinée d'après les quatre évangélistes et répartie sur les heures de tierce, sexte et none, devait être d'un usage assez général, car on la retrouve en plusieurs lectionnaires." (*Le Lectionnaire*, IX, 44.)

63. *Acta Apostolorum Apocrypha post Constantinum Tischendorf,* denuo ediderunt Ricardus Adelbertus Lipsius et Maximilianus Bonnet, 2 vols. (Lipsiae: Hermannum Mendelssohn, 1891–98), I, 118–77.

64. Salmon, VII, lxxvi.

65. Lipsius has a separate study of the Marcellus–text in *Die Apokryphen Apostelgeschichten und Apostellegenden,* 3 vols. in 4 (Braunschweig: C. A. Schwetschke, 1883–90), II, 284ff.

66. Ibid., pp. 284–85. A Greek manuscript of the story was discovered in 1490 by Constantinus Laskaris at the monastery of S. Maria di Trapizonata in Sicily. St. Paul is said to have visited the Sicilian town of Messina on his way to Rome and to have ordained its first bishop (p. 285).

67. Lipsius, *Acta,* I, 119.

censure of his colleague if he is found to deserve it. A heated argument between the recently converted Christians and the Jewish faction absorbs much of the account into a forensic rhetoric with little narrative content. Like the story of Julian and Basilissa, the legend serves as a vehicle for the exposition of controversial doctrines and rituals, such as occupied the early Church in its initial stages. Consequently, the style is dialogic in a kind of antiphonal interaction of speech constructs. Paul succeeds in calming the turbulence through his citation of Old Testament passages, and many of the Jewish adherents accept Christianity.

The central phase of the narrative involves the claim by Simon Magus to be the Son of God, as he performs marvels in rivalry with the miracles wrought by Peter. The conflict draws the attention of the Roman Emperor Nero, who holds a public inquest, at which Peter and his rival resume the earlier debate that had marked Paul's arrival. Simon sends raving dogs against his opponent, who calms them with bread that he had concealed in the sleeves of his tunic (p. 143). The *tour de force* occurs when Simon predicts that he will ascend into heaven. Having constructed a high tower in preparation for the event, he succeeds in flying from it, but at Peter's prayer he falls to the ground and is broken into fragments.

Nero proceeds to imprison Peter and Paul, and after a time orders his prefect Agrippa to arrange their execution. The latter advises beheading for Paul, whom he regards as innocent, but crucifixion for Peter. As the two deaths are administered, Peter closes the narrative with a short homily to his followers, before the crucifixion, head downward by his choice, that constitutes his martyrdom (pp. 171–73).

The dialogic form of the legend, like that of Julian and Basilissa, was eminently suited to public recitative or chanting and indicates an audience deeply involved in both heroic narrative and forensic oratory. The very length of the two pieces (thirty and fifty modern printed pages) suggests the division of the material into several distinct lections, for the solemn Matins office and the Mass itself. Although there is no rubric in either case giving explicit directions for the apportionment of the narrative, Dom Salmon favors the division of these legends between the "hours" of the Divine Office and the Mass.[68] He cites the corresponding Spanish custom,[69] and compares with it the practice of reading the Passion of Christ on Good Friday in three segments, at Tierce, Sext, and None, attested by Gallican lectionaries.[70]

The narrative of these forensic debates and heroic sufferings suggests the kind of epic struggle that appealed to early medieval audiences. The Gallican era was one of barbaric folk wandering, conquest, conversion to Christianity and political-religious persecution. The chanted recitative of the hagiographical *vita* was a phenomenon closely analogous to the celebration of a great warrior's deeds by the *scop* at the Germanic banquet hall, and scholarly opinion has long favored the relationship of saint's life to *chanson de geste*.[71] Moreover, the detailed accounts of doctrinal controversy, often debated in the presence of a pagan Roman administrator conducting the saint's trial, spoke to the semi-barbaric Christian congregations who were themselves only a little removed from their pagan outlooks and pagan deities. It is not difficult to understand why the congregations then attending Matins and Mass regarded the essential core of religion and liturgy to be the lections. This overshadowing of the Eucharistic action by public recitation at the saint's festival characterized the Gallican and Hispanic liturgies, but it is thoroughly understandable in its historical context.[72]

The Hispanic liturgy gives evidence of a comparable interest

---

68. On the division of the St. Julian *passio*, see Salmon, VII, 27 ff. He also discusses the use of the *Passio Petri et Pauli* in the Mass as replacement for the Old Testament "prophetic" lection, preceding the day's Epistle (*Rom.* 8:15–27) and the Gospel (Matt. 5:1–16). (Ibid.)

69. Salmon, IX, 56; 59–60.   70. See above, n. 62.

71. Faral, *Les Jongleurs*, pp. 46–48.   72. Porter, *The Gallican Rite*, p. 51.

in public recitation of saints' lives during the Visigothic era (sixth and seventh centuries). The *liber commicus,* as defined above in Chapter II, was the Spanish equivalent of the Gallican *lectionarium* and had many of the same features separating it from contemporary Roman books of this type. The three Mass lections here were the prophetic, Apostolic, and Evangelical, with the occasional replacement of the first and second by a saint's life. In Fray Justo Perez de Urbel's edition of the surviving *liber commicus* versions, he prints only one of the several sanctoral lections of this type scattered among the manuscript texts of Silos, León, San Millán de la Cogolla, and Toledo. Strictly speaking, this one is not a *vita,* but is the account of many miracles worked at the intercession of St. Stephen in North Africa, where St. Augustine composed the account as part of his *De Civitate Dei,* Book 22. The extract from Augustine's work is contained in the Silos manuscript of the *liber commicus* and also in the Cardeña manuscript of the *Pasionario hispanico.*[73]

Augustine had figured prominently in the propagation of St. Stephen's cult because relics of the saint were brought to him by Orosius, who was present in Jerusalem when Stephen's tomb was miraculously discovered at Cafargamala in 415. A number of North African churches received relics at the time, for example, at Uzali, where Stephen's fame grew through the marvelous occurrences taking place there. Augustine himself was present at the miraculous cure of Petronia, a matron of Uzali, and on his recommendation she wrote an account of the event for an official *libellus* that would be read publicly to assembled congregations ("ortati sumus . . . ut libellum daret, qui recitaretur in populo, et obedientissime paruit").[74] Augustine refers repeatedly to this practice of making a formal deposition concerning a miracle so that the facts would be preserved for the

---

73. *De Civitate Dei,* XXII, viii, 10–22. See Perez de Urbel, *Liber Commicus,* I, 25–30; A. Fábrega Grau, *Pasionario hispanico,* II, 78–83.

74. *Liber Commicus,* I, 28.

edification of those who had not witnessed the event, and could be read to them.[75]

Among other wonders of this kind contained in Augustine's account are the cure of a blind woman during a procession in which the bishop was carrying relics of Stephen; restoration to life of the priest, Eucherius; the resuscitation of a small child crushed to death beneath the wheel of an ox-cart; and the deathbed conversion to Christianity of Martial, a prominent citizen. In this last case, Martial's daughter and son-in-law had become Christians and had entreated him in vain to embrace their new faith. After prayers to Stephen at his shrine, the son-in-law brought a piece of the flower arrangement from the altar, placed it upon the dying man's head and experienced the awakening of Martial with a request for Baptism.[76]

The most elaborately narrated miracle in the series is the last one. It concerns a brother and sister afflicted with a kind of palsy, who come to Augustine shortly before Easter to seek his counsel and to pray at the shrine of St. Stephen. On Easter Sunday, Paulus, the young boy, falls into a swoon while praying before the reliquary, and arises from the experience cured of his illness. The people present with him rush with the news to Augustine, who then speaks in his sermon of the day about the marvelous power of God, and leads them in reflection on the miracle. A few days later he reads the official *libellus* to the congregation, in the presence of the two young people. Palladia, the sister, has not been cured, but after the public reading she hastens again to the reliquary and prays to Stephen while Augustine is still speaking about the earlier miracle. She experiences the kind of swoon or sleep that Paulus had undergone, and arises cured as he had been.[77]

The practice of public reading in the case of a miraculous event seems to have been of Augustine's own making, but it

75. Ibid., pp. 28–30.
77. Ibid., pp. 29–30.

76. Ibid., Miracle IV, p. 26.

serves as a paradigm that may be the origin of the whole structure appearing in the later liturgy of saints' days. Fábrega Grau says it is not certain when this extract from the *De Civitate Dei* became a lection in the Spanish liturgy for Stephen's feast day, but that probably its incorporation occurred in the fifth to sixth century, that is, around the year 500.[78] Salmon says that churches in Spain and Italy obtained relics of St. Stephen soon after the churches in northern Africa had received them from Orosius and that churches in Gaul must also have secured relics, as many edifices came to be dedicated to Stephen.[79] Dom Germain Morin, in his edition of the Silos *Liber Commicus*, comments on the lection that is extracted from *De Civitate Dei* and observes that the custom of reading *passiones* or saints' *vitae* at Mass "recepta erat in Ecclesia Gallicana et in Mediolanensi. . . . in Toletana quoque provincia,"[80] but he gives no chronological indication for the origin of the custom.

The life of St. Martin, discussed above in note 57 from a bibliographical perspective, is a late insertion into the Spanish liturgy. It contains famous incidents from Martin's spectacular life, for example, the dividing of his cloak with an unclothed beggar, amid jeers and laughter from casual witnesses at the ridiculous appearance of the truncated mantle. There is the incident of his own miraculous recovery from grave illness caused by his consumption of hellebore, a poisonous plant, during his exile and pursuit by Arian enemies. The work of destroying pagan temples, often against the resistance of hostile crowds, is a prominent feature; and incidents of healing the sick occur, the most spectacular being the cure of a leper by kissing his diseased face.[81]

The manuscript supplement to the Silos *Liber Commicus* (now

---

78. Fábrega Grau, I, 194.
79. Salmon, *Le Lectionnaire*, IX, 39 (citing É. Mâle, *La Fin du paganisme en Gaule*, p. 227).
80. Morin, ed. *Liber Commicus*, p. 20.
81. Sulpicius Severus, *Opera*, I, 113–27.

known as Arch. Mon. 3) contains a short lection for the feast of the Assumption of Mary, taken from the "Canticle of Canticles," and another narrating her death and assumption. The latter includes the attack upon Mary's funeral procession by some hostile Jewish people, their punishment by being stricken with deformity, and their miraculous healing. Férotin has edited these two texts[82] and observes that the narrative one recalls the work attributed to Melito of Sardis, *De Transitu Virginis Mariae* (p. 795).

The life of St. Aemilian by Bishop Braulio is probably the most significant evidence of the Spanish custom in the Visigothic era. This is the San Millán de la Cogolla of the great abbey by that name. Jean Mabillon regarded the *vita* as strong evidence of the public reading in Spain and of its occurrence in the Mass of the saint's festival. "Certe," he wrote, "Hispani vitas sanctorum . . . in sacris etiam publicis recitabant, ut luculenter inter alia probat Braulionis Caesaraugustani episcopi libellus de gestis beati Aemiliani abbatis, quem libellum ideo conscripsit 'ut posset in missae ejus celebratione quantocius legi,' quemadmodum Braulio ipse in Praefatione sua loquitur."[83] The *libellus* was written by Braulio, Bishop of Saragossa in the mid-seventh century, at the urging of close associates who were conscious of the great popularity of Aemilian among the Spaniards as an ascetic and miracle-worker. The preface referred to above is a public letter prefixed to his *libellus* and addressed to the Bishop's brother Fronimian. Braulio is saying that he has made the *vita* a short one so that it could be used to any desired extent as a Mass lection for the feast.[84]

---

82. *Liber Mozarabicus Sacramentorum*, VI, 786–95. Férotin gives no account of the sixth-century Eastern text, the "pseudo-Melito" (the so-called *Transitus B*) nor of the Assumption literature related to it. For a survey of this literature see Catherine Louise Wall, "A Study of 'The Appearance of Our Lady to Thomas,' Pageant XLVI in the York Cycle of Mystery Plays," diss. The Catholic University of America, 1965, pp. 5–13.

83. Mabillon, *DLG*, Col. 122, 20–21.

84. *Sancti Braulionis Caesaraugustani Episcopi Vita S. Emiliani*, ed. Luis Vazquez de Parga, 2d ed. (Madrid: Consejo Superior de Investigaciones Científicas,

Braulio was one of the learned bishops of seventh-century Spain, and, distinguished as a man of letters, had been a monk before his call to the episcopacy. He made Saragossa a great intellectual center in his day, in an age marked by an unusual collaboration of monastic centers with outstanding leaders in the episcopate, a feature that had distinguished Gaul in the fifth and sixth centuries but was not to be found except in Spain during the seventh century.[85] In the life of Aemilian he carefully directed his little book to a popular audience, soliciting devout religious attention and warning that one should not come to the hearing eager for eloquence but for edification: "Non hic uerborum plenum auidum, sed religione plenum praebeat auditum" (p. 12.) If the people were not willing to accept this challenge, he advised them to withdraw and not to waste their time on the lection.

The account that Braulio gives of Aemilian's life is simple and straightforward, as there are only a few events in the story.[86] Having chosen the occupation of a shepherd, the young man planned to while away his time playing the cithara as he watched the sheep, but soon had a vision in which he was called to abandon this chosen work for the spiritually contemplative life.[87] He committed himself to the care of a hermit named Felix, in order to undergo an initiation into asceticism. After this period of preparation he withdrew to a place near

---

1943), p. 5. The reading in Vazquez's edition of Braulio's statement is: "breuem conscripsi, ut possit in missae eius celebritate quantocius legi. . . ." *Quantocius* most probably is to be read as the word that the *Oxford Latin Dictionary* spells *quantusuis*, meaning "of whatever size, amount, degree, etc." (Oxford: Clarendon Press, 1968), II, 1542. For an account of the way by which Aemilian's name became connected with the Abbey of San Millán de la Cogolla see *The Book of Saints*, ed. by the Benedictine Monks of St. Augustine's Abbey, Ramsgate, 5th ed. (New York: Thomas Crowell, 1966), p. 233.

85. Riché, *Education and Culture*, p. 298.

86. Vazquez, in his critical edition cited above (n. 84), indicates that several of the nine manuscripts used are those of a complete office for the saint's day and the others are copies of a hagiographical collection attributed to a monk of the late Visigothic era named Valerio.

87. *Vita S. Emiliani*, p. 14, 8.

Vergegio, but finding it too easily accessible to the number of people who sought him out, he changed his eremitical abode to a remote spot high on Mt. Dercecio, where he remained forty years (pp. 15–16). Summoned at this late age in life by Dimidio, Bishop of Tarazona, he was ordained for the diocese and assigned to a pastorate in the town where he had first located, Vergegio. Aemilian administered his parish by giving away much of its financial possession to the poor, for which activity he was denounced to the bishop. Dimidio angrily relieved him of his assignment and left him free to return to his hermitage (pp. 19–20). His fame as a miracle-worker before and after his death attracted great renown to him, and a number of the miracles are related by Braulio to conclude the *vita* (pp. 20–32). To this solitary contemplative and the disciples who gathered around him is attributed the origin of the famous monastery bearing his name.[88]

Reflection on the process of public reading in the sixth to eighth centuries may suggest a recapitulation of several features: the extraordinary, festive context of a pilgrimage shrine; the presence of a presiding bishop revealing the secular (i.e., diocesan) nature of the ceremony; the permeation of the day's liturgy by the saint's life (both in brief summaries of the *contestatio* or *inlatio* and in the full-scale *vita* read in divisions of moderate length at the Matins vigils); and finally in the Mass itself, where the prophetic and apostolic readings would have been replaced by the sanctoral one. The tension of the occasion was twofold, consisting primarily in a narrative of heroic deeds, miracles, and suffering; secondarily in the atmosphere of hopeful expectancy for the occurrence of a visible miracle on the spot among the faithful gathered at the shrine. Given the background of semi-barbaric life in the Visigothic era with its folk-wanderings, battles, conquests, and persecutions, the narratives read aloud had something of the tribal splendor of epic

88. See above, n. 84.

about them, and the lector himself possessed something of the bard in his make-up, perhaps even the professional training of *juglaría*. Little wonder, then, that the oral performance should overshadow the sacramental and sacrificial structure of the Eucharistic liturgy, as W. S. Porter laments, and that the chanting of the Divine Office of Matins might become a parodic rendering of psalmody in the singing and dance of the gathered crowd, shocking a Caesarius or an Eligius. What emerges in the foreground is the picture of the Mediterranean tradition at a festival of the gods: a story told in recitative and prompting an accompaniment of *choreia* and *saltationes*, at least in some places. Spain holds the key to the full understanding of this well-intentioned *contrafactum, a lo divino,* that sometimes called forth the official condemnation of a church council upon it.

CHAPTER V

LITURGICAL DANCE AS SACRED DRAMA: THE HISPANIC PARADIGM

Although the public reading of saints' lives in the Gallic liturgies, discussed in the preceding chapter, is well documented as a recitative performance, the accompaniment of the hagiographical lection by formal dramatic action is less clear. The thesis that the Roman mime underlies this paraliturgical celebration has to be worked out through the phenomenon of sacred dance, as the usual form of the pagan mime in a Christian context. Liturgical dance has always been a fragile experiment in pastoral practice, capable of reverent and hieratic realization but subject to abuse by its very association with the pagan tradition. As Dom Gougaud, the Benedictine historian, once wrote, the medieval local clergy organized the use of dance in parish celebrations, but church authority in such cases tolerated rather than approved the custom and it was never an official practice in the universal Church.[1] To miss the significance of sacred dance where it did occur, however, is to lose the thread of continuity in the history of drama, because dance gesture is a symbolic, stylized form of impersonation and an essential element in the southern European history of theater. Here the strongest evidence comes from Spain.

The principle of the *contrafactum* (*a lo divino*), discussed in Chapter III, nowhere has a clearer realization than in Hispanic dance, as a transformation of pagan theatrical technique. Spain

---

1. L. Gougaud, "La Danse dans les églises," *Revue d'histoire ecclésiastique*, 15 (1914), 7.

was alone among European countries in possessing both a popular folk dance and an institutionalized form sponsored by the
Church itself through its cathedral life. The latter practice consisted in the training of young boys for professional execution
of dance at high religious festivals, in a special program of education designed for a small group of youths. The term by which
the boys came to be known was the *seises* (because six of them
were selected and educated separately from other students of
the cathedral school).[2] This formal program of training in sacred
dance must be distinguished from popular dance (*el baile*),
which was connected with parish life and folk festival,[3] but the
great esteem in which the boy choristers and dancers were held
for centuries served to give an aura of respectability to liturgical
dance in Spain, much stronger there than in other European
countries.

Spain produced a medieval Latin liturgical drama only in a
very restricted area, Catalonia. This was the territory conquered
by Charlemagne's armies and subjected to the Roman liturgical
rite that had been imposed already upon Gaul in the mid-eighth
century. Central and Western Spain apparently had no such
drama, as surviving Latin texts of Easter and Christmas plays
are extremely rare in Castile and other neighboring areas, and
are virtually nonexistent in Portugal as well.[4] Spanish historians
have often expressed the opinion that such a drama came to
non-Catalonian Spain after the imposition there of the Roman
rite in 1081, nearly three centuries after Charlemagne. Cluniac
influence from France was strong in the establishment of this
liturgical reform in the late eleventh century, and Cluniac encouragement there of the Latin drama has been favored as a

2. Richard Donovan, *The Liturgical Drama in Medieval Spain*, p. 38.
3. Juan Moraleda y Esteban, *Los Seises de la Catedral de Toledo* (Toledo: A. Garijo, 1911), pp. 15, 35, 62. It is not perfectly clear from Moraleda's account, but
he seems to indicate that the name *seises* is a late usage (sixteenth century).
4. Father Donovan has given a whole chapter (6) to the reasons for this great
lacuna in Spanish liturgical texts and has recorded the work that Solange Corbin
did in Portugal, revealing virtually nothing there of Latin liturgical drama.

scholarly hypothesis. Father Richard Donovan has shown, however, that liturgical plays never flourished in Cluniac houses in France, and that such encouragement in Spain by them is extremely improbable. His own conclusion is that Latin liturgical plays did not penetrate the large Castilian area, and that only in the late Middle Ages this territory came to possess a sacred drama; moreover, that it was a vernacular Spanish, not Latin, theater when it did appear.[5]

The view I offer takes into account this absence of Latin liturgical drama in non-Catalonian Spain. Moreover, it takes into account the problem of proving a secular dramatic tradition there. Those who have favored a continuity of the ancient Roman comic tradition in Spain, above all Bonilla y San Martin,[6] have admitted that surviving texts even of a secular, profane theater cannot be produced as evidence of continuity. My proposition is therefore that the texts needed to prove the existence of either secular or religious drama are the saints' lives, in the *liber commicus* and the legendaries, and that these were dramatized in the recitative with mimic dance that belong to the ancient Roman tradition. No one has, to my knowledge, made this suggestion, and it is a radical approach to the historical puzzle. Castile, I maintain, had no need of a liturgical Latin drama because it possessed an ancient, more popular tradition in its own heritage, a heritage that it shared with southern Gaul until about 750, and that it preserved for three hundred years longer because it had not been required to accept the Latin liturgical reform of the Carolingian era.

The longevity of the Spanish dance tradition is its most re-

5. Donovan, pp. 69–70. The classic study of this whole problem of the Roman rite in Catalonia is Higini Anglès, *La Música a Catalunya fins al segle XIII* (Barcelona: Institut d'Estudis Catalans, 1935).

6. Adolfo Bonilla y San Martin, *Las Bacantes o del origen de teatro*, pp. 35–42; Juan Hurtado and J. de la Serna, *Historia de la literatura española* (Madrid: SAETA, 1949), p. 96. On the other hand, Deyermond dismisses the whole idea of a lost Roman tradition in the Spanish drama (*A Literary History of Spain: The Middle Ages* [London: Ernest Benn; New York: Barnes and Noble, 1971], p. 206.)

markable feature. It is at least as old as Roman civilization in Spain, and it is still alive today. The *seises* even now continue their solemn dance in the diocese of Seville and I have myself seen a performance of the popular *baile* in Majorca (on the vigil of the Assumption of Mary, August 14).[7] Juan Moraleda y Esteban, in detailing the history of the cathedral *seises* in Toledo, makes a strong case for the unbroken continuity of sacred dance from the earliest Christian centuries in Spain, the days of the Roman Empire. He sees this practice as a transference of pagan technique to a Christian use. A Graeco-Roman set of customs lives on through the Visigothic and Mozarabic centuries and flowers more profusely after the reconquest of Spain from the Moors. He expresses his general view in favor of "la persistencia de las costumbres romanas y greco-romanas en la sociedad visigoda, y por ende en su sucesora la mozárabe. . . ."[8] Moreover, he makes two points very emphatically: (1) that the Christian adaptation of Roman dance was a reverent and sacred occurrence, not an abuse; and (2) that the custom could not have originated as a practice during the Moorish supremacy in Spain (after 711) because Christians lived a precarious existence under Moorish rule and could not have created an original, experimental phenomenon in a context of persecution.[9] Christians

7. Donovan, p. 38. A chance piece of information about modern dancing on saints' days came to me from a child in Brazil, whom I know through an educational program sponsored by the National Council of Catholic Women in Washington. The boy, Silvio Alessandro, in an informal letter to me written on June 16, 1987, mentioned among recent events the June Festivals of three saints (Anthony, John the Baptist, and Peter) celebrated in public squares decorated with paper pennants and flags. Of considerable interest to me was his remark that the celebrations include square dancing (*quadrilha*) by organized groups of *dançarinos*. I quote from his letter in the Brazilian Portuguese: ". . . neste mês inicia-se as festas juninas, são comemorações que se fazem em homenagem a 3 santos (Santo Antônio, dia 13; são João, 24 e São Pedro, dia 29), as festas são realizadas em terreiros (áreas de terras), enfeitados com bandeirolas de papel, para a realização dos eventos. Existem também danças organizadas com grupos de dançarinos, que nós chamamos de 'quadrilha.'"

8. Moraleda, pp. 70–71.

9. Ibid., p. 14.

under Arab rule, he insists, were simply allowed to continue this custom from earlier centuries, and they bequeathed it to their descendants. (H. Anglès makes essentially the same case for Mozarabic music as a type already established in Visigothic Spain and continued, not created, during Arabic rule.[10])

Although Moraleda does not use the term "a lo divino," it is clear that he treats the early Christian dance in this sense, as a *contrafactum*. "Los primeros cristianos de la ciudad de Tajo [the Tagus River area, central Spain] danzaron también en honor del mártir del Gólgota y de su Santa Madre, así como para festejar el recuerdo de los confesores, las vírgenes y los mártires, seguidores de la doctrina del Nazareno Jesús, y estas Danzas tenían lugar dentro y fuera de los Templos."[11]

Although religious dance was associated with various church feast days in Spain, its connection with saints' festivals was especially close. The records of conciliar decrees in both Spain and Gaul make this point very clear. What happened was a case of historical irony. The devotion to the saints was encouraged by the bishops in both countries as a way of freeing the people from pagan superstitions and of teaching Christian holiness to them.[12] These festivals then became the focus of ancient practices that simply persisted in the dancing and singing groups, forcing the ecclesiastical leaders to condemn them and prompting conciliar decrees against desecration of the sanctoral festivals. A similar experience had already occurred in the churches of the Eastern Mediterranean, as indicated above. It had also played a part in the North African ecclesiastical life revealed in

---

10. H. Anglès, "Latin Chant before St. Gregory," *The New Oxford History of Music* (London: Oxford University Press, 1955), II, 83.

11. Moraleda, p. 62.

12. H. G. J. Beck, *The Pastoral Care of Souls in South-East France during the Sixth Century* (Rome: Gregorian University Press, 1950), pp. 307–08; J. N. Hillgarth, "Popular Religion in Visigothic Spain," in *Visigothic Spain: New Approaches*, ed. Edward James (Oxford: Clarendon Press, 1980), p. 51; É. Mâle, *La Fin du paganisme en Gaul*, pp. 54–69; Salmon, IX, 65–66.

the Third Council of Carthage, and in Augustine's preoccupation with abuses of this kind.

The historical records of dancing as an integral part of the saint's festival are usually negative in their import. They are accounts of abuse and condemnations of such abuse, rather than testimony to encouragement of the practice. Official records, alas, are often made not of eulogy or encouragement but of censure and disapproval. The positive aspect of the historical event, the slow growth of a devout religious custom (even if capable of abuse) tends to go without notice in conciliar files. It does, however, serve to reveal in the present case the customs of an era and their tenacity among the people in spite of condemnation and censure.

There were three conciliar condemnations from Gaul and Spain in the Visigothic era, even though there was a more receptive attitude among the Hispanic ecclesiastical authorities to the dance phenomenon. They were Auxerre (573), Toledo III (589), and Chalon (639). Nevertheless, the best known of these decrees is that of the third Toledan council. Although this gathering was predominantly concerned with the Arian heresy and its abjuration by the Visigothic king of Spain, Recared, and by his people,[13] Canon XXIII thunders explicitly against the irreverence and the uproar of celebrations connected with the saints' festivals. It thus becomes a paradigm for official attitudes of the period. J. Vives quotes its provisions:

Exterminanda omnino est inreligiosa consuetudo quam vulgus *per sanctorum sollemnitates* agere consuevit, ut populi qui debent officia divina adtendere saltationibus et turpibus invigilent canticis, non solum sibi nocentes sed et religiosorum officiis perstrepentes: hoc enim ut ab omni Spania depellatur, sacerdotum et judicum a concilio sancto curae conmittitur. [Emphasis supplied.][14]

13. Ricardo Garcia Villoslada, ed., *Historia de la iglesia en España* (Madrid: Biblioteca de Autores Cristianos, 1979), I, 409–13.

14. *Concilios Visigóticos e Hispano-Romanos*, ed. José Vives (Barcelona-Madrid: Consejo Superior de Investigaciones Científicas, Instituto Enrique Flórez, 1963), I, 27.

The heading for this decree is: "Ut in sanctorum natalitiis bal-lemaciae prohibeantur." J. Fernández Alonso, in his study of pastoral care during the Visigothic era, quotes the above decree and observes that the condemned practices must have been deeply rooted indeed, and widespread, for a national council to take up the matter and to align both ecclesiastical and civil power ("sacerdotum et judicum") against them.[15] The wording of the prohibition indicates that authentic clerical recitation of the Divine Office was the normal way of celebrating the saint's festival, and that the people were competing with the chanting of the office (Matins surely), and were disturbing the sacred ob-servance by the uproar of their singing and dancing.

The Council of Auxerre had spoken in similar terms about fifteen years earlier. It was concerned with practices of pagan superstition associated with vigil services, for example, with prayers offered at fountains or trees that had traditions of pagan cult. The synod made explicit reference, however, to saints' vig-ils. In Canon III it declared: "Non licet compensus [oblations] in domibus propriis nec peruigilius [sic] in festivitates sanctorum facere. . . ."[16] In an even more particularized prohibition (Canon V), it forbade vigils in honor of St. Martin: "Omnino inter supra dictis conditionibus peruigilius, quos in honore Martini obser-uant, omnimodis prohibite." (Ibid.) That these vigil celebrations

---

15. Justo Fernández Alonso, *La Cura pastoral en la España romano-visigoda* (Ma-drid: Estades, Artes Gráficas, 1955), p. 351.

16. *Concilia Galliae, A. 511–A.695,* ed. Carolus de Clercq, *Corpus Christianorum, Series Latina* (Turnhout, Belgium: Brepols, 1963), Vol. 148A, p. 265. Several of the words here need special glossing. Du Cange has a long article on "compensus," in which he quotes this passage from the Council of Auxerre. One meaning is that of a pile of wool or yarn to be offered by a woman on a saint's vigil, appar-ently to invoke the saint's assistance in the woman's tasks of weaving. The sec-ond meaning, more relevant here, is that of making oblations in private homes on vigils rather than attending church services, or after attending them. This practice seems to retain about it some trace of ancient rituals for household gods. (*Glossarium Mediae et Infimae Latinitatis,* rev. ed. Léopold Favre (Paris: Librairie des Sciences et des Arts, 1937), II, 464. "Compensus" and "pervigilius" are here to be construed, apparently, as masculine accusative plurals, although "pervigi-lia" was a neuter plural in Late Latin. See *The Oxford Latin Dictionary.*

involved singing and dance is made probable by Canon IX: "Non licet in ecclesia chorus saecularium uel puellarum cantica exercere nec conuiuia in ecclesia praeparare. . . ." (p. 266).

The Council of Chalon (c. 650) dealt in Canon XIX with abuse of public ceremonies at church dedications and at the feasts of martyrs. Marignan had cited this decree in his study of saints' festivals in Gaul, and the language is notable for its close similarity to that of Auxerre a century earlier: "Valde omnibus nuscetur [let it be known] esse decretum, ne per dedicationes basilicarum aut festiuitates martyrum ad ipsa solemnia confluentes obscina et turpea cantica, dum orare debent aut clericus psallentes audire, cum choris foemineis, turpia quidem, decantare uideantur."[17] The prohibition is accompanied by the assertion that such practices of choral performance are forbidden in the cathedral enclosure and on the porches, and that those who persist in these *cantica* are to be punished by excommunication. The juncture of *cantica* with *choris foemineis* clearly denotes dance, as the word *chorus* had from classical Roman times the meaning of dance;[18] and the Greek Χορεία was the term in the Byzantine period for a poem accompanied by dance in mimed form,[19] as Vénétia Cottas discusses it. The word *cantica* itself, occurring in these canonical decrees, has of course the meaning of song, but it also had a long association with Roman comic drama. As early as the work of Plautus, the term indicated lyrical passages embedded in a play, and in Late Latin it occurs again and again in relation to dance activity. The terminology of a later council's decree, that of Avignon in 1209, continues to associate song and dance, explicitly prohibiting their use at saints' vigils, in language similar to that of the sixth and seventh centuries: "Statuimus, ut in *sanctorum vigiliis* in ecclesiis histori-

---

17. *Concilia Galliae*, Vol. 148A, p. 307.

18. (*Oxford Latin Dictionary*, I, 311.)

19. Vénétia Cottas defines the Greek Χορεία as a "poème dansé et chanté," and again as "un simple poème destiné à être dansé mimiquement sur la scène." (*Le Théâtre à Byzance*, p. 48; *Oxford Latin Dictionary*, I, 311.)

cae saltationes, obscoeni motus, seu choreae non fiant, nec dicantur amatoria carmina, vel cantilenae ibidem; ex quibus praeter id quod aliquotiens auditorum animi ad immunditiam provocantur, obturus [read obtutus, "seeing"] & auditus quorumlibet spectantium polluuntur."[20] The "historicae saltationes" are probably mimed or danced narratives, and the other terms, "motus," "choreae," and "carmina" are congruent with this interpretation. Alfaric, studying this decree of Avignon, translates "historicae saltationes" as "danses théâtrales," revealing his own conviction that a dramatic performance is in question.[21]

The evidence from conciliar decrees in the early Middle Ages, as we have seen, is a testimony to the close association between the celebration of saints' vigils and the ancient pagan customs in honor of the Roman gods. The witness of individual ecclesiastical authorities, such as local bishops and pastors, tells the same story as the conciliar decrees and often does it in a more revealing manner than the formal proclamations of church councils. Historians have recorded the struggles of bishops to persuade their people in celebrating saints' vigils and other religious festivals to avoid the abuses that had become associated with these occasions. Among such careful shepherds of the semi-barbaric congregations in Visigothic religious circumstances, Caesarius of Arles is of great significance for this historical phenomenon, and also for the development of the Gallic liturgies of his native Gaul and contemporary Spain. The rhetorical *address* of these individual statements is one of pastoral persuasion to restraint or piety in celebration rather than ad-

20. Mansi, "Concilium Avenionense," Vol. XXII, Cols. 791–92. Emphasis supplied.

21. Alfaric and Hoepffner, eds. *La Chanson de Ste. Foy,* 2 vols. (London: Oxford University Press, 1928), II, 74. Alfaric's interest in the citation is in its testimony to mimed song, which he himself wished to prove in the vernacular *Chanson* performed at the pilgrimage shrine in Conques. "Historia" as a narrative or story is recorded in the *Oxford Latin Dictionary,* I, 799, from Plautus to Aulus Gellius. Alexander Souter's *Glossary of Later Latin to 600 A.D.* gives as one of the meanings for the adjective "historicus–a–um" the term "theatrical" (Oxford: Clarendon Press, 1949), p. 175.

ministrative legislation forbidding abuse and threatening punishment.

The observance of St. John Baptist's Nativity and the feast of
St. Martial were of special concern to ecclesiastical leaders in
Gaul because of the context surrounding these two days. Caesarius discussed the feast of St. John Baptist's Nativity (June 24)
in Sermon 216. The occurrence of the summer solstice at this
time made the saint's festival particularly vulnerable to pagan
traditions. The "St. John Fires" associated with this day developed from ancient fire dances, sometimes using torches, that
had been regarded as purifying the land, foliage, and cattle of
harmful vapors and insects.[22] The vigil had become a focus of
highly objectionable carousing; Caesarius urged his congregations to avoid scurrilous language in songs on this day, and to
prepare in a devout spirit for its proper observance by fast-
ing and by preserving peace with neighbors.[23] Specifically he
pleaded with those having household authority to forbid their
relatives and retinue from engaging in the offending public
cantica on this day: "Nec permittamus voluptuosos quosque
solemnitatem sanctam cantica luxoriosa proferendo polluere"
(p. 861.).

The festival of St. John received explicit regulation again in
the seventh century from Eligius, Bishop of Noyon and missionary to northern and eastern Gaul.[24] In the life of this vigorous
evangelizer, written by Audoenus (St. Ouen), the biographer
says that Eligius fought against pagan practices among his
people and specifically decreed: "Nullus in festivatate sancti Io-
hannis vel quibusque sanctorum sollemnitatibus solestitia aut
vallationes [read "ballationes"] vel saltationes aut cantica dia-

22. Renée Foatelli, *Les Danses religieuses dans la christianisme*, pp. 36–37.
23. Caesarius, Sermon 216 (Morin, rev. ed. II, 861). Dom Morin, who has
sifted the sermons of Caesarius to determine their use of earlier writers like St.
Augustine, regards the ending of Sermon 216, the passage here in question, as
Caesarius' own work, although the piece as a whole is a cento of various ecclesiastical writers. (Ibid., p. 858.)
24. Riché, *Education and Culture*, pp. 214, 330 n. 134.

bolica exerceat."[25] Although the prohibition covers all saints' festivals, it makes its point in relation to the St. John context, which R. Foatelli says has always been a major item in the popular culture of Provence. The *vita* of Eligius records the peculiar irony that on one occasion the bishop, while preaching against pagan superstitions, was attacked by the hostile congregation, some of whom broke into *dance*.[26]

Comparable to the St. John's day customs and creating some of the same problems were the celebrations of St. Marcel's festival (St. Martial), but I discuss them later as examples of the favorable reception of dance in ecclesiastical contexts because they seem to have fared rather well.

The formal denunciations of dance activity in ecclesiastical contexts and the ambivalence between formal decree and actual practice are puzzling. Father A. de Parvillez, a Jesuit priest, wrote an introductory essay for the historical survey of religious dance by Foatelli, in which he observed that the Church condemned only abuses, not the phenomenon itself: "L'Église en blâmant les abus, n'a jamais interdit l'usage raisonnable; en émondant l'arbre elle ne prétend pas le déraciner." The name of Caesarius, which seems to reappear in every phase of the historical development of saints' festivals, scarcely seems to be associated with merely "pruning the tree." Must we think of him as an exceptionally puritanical spirit battling without compromise against a pagan tradition? I am inclined rather to think of him as a special figure in the controversy, situated in a strategic administrative position affecting the Church in both Gaul and Spain. Although he seems neutral to the public reading of saints' lives and hostile toward the use of dance, his own solutions to the problem seem to have been vigorously creative and

25. "Vita Eligii Episcopi Noviomagensis," ed. Bruno Krusch, *MGH* (*Scriptores Rerum Merovingicarum*. Hannoverae et Lipsiae: Impensis Bibliopolii Hahniani, 1902), IV, 705–06. Du Cange, I, 532, indicates that "ballationes" and "vallationes" are valid spellings for this word meaning "dances."
26. Krusch, pp. 711–12, and Riché, p. 492.

deserve special consideration below to arrive at a total estimate.

Foatelli, who has given probably the best analysis of the favorable Old Testament references to religious dance, explains that the love of this prayerful, rhythmic activity is a distinctive attribute of Hebraic people and is a special manifestation of that "chaleur orientale" characteristic of all the countries of the Levant (p. 20). The generally receptive attitude of Spanish tradition to this phenomenon needs to be understood in part as Biblical tradition and in part as a pagan Roman one. Prosper Alfaric sees the conciliar decrees as giving the impression that the singing and dancing at the vigils was completely a pagan custom. He argues, to the contrary, that such purely pagan festivity could not have entered into the sanctoral celebrations. It would not have passed through the churchyard gates on that basis. Rather, dance must have been a mixture of pagan and Christian elements from the beginning, and the composite must have been undertaken and permitted as a well-intentioned act of devotion. "Tout porte à croire," he insists, "qu'elles [the dance and the songs] constituaient plutôt une sorte de liturgie populaire correspondant à celle du clergé. C'était par dévotion que l'on ajoutait aux chants et aux gestes préscrits par l'Église d'autres gestes et d'autres chants d'un caractère plus libre."[27] This composite activity, I would add, was preserved for hundreds of years in Spanish life, not only at the popular level, but also in the formal context of cathedral culture. To a more limited extent this kind of *contrafactum* was permitted in other Western European countries, but records of it are rare and scattered. The Spanish institution was the paradigm and was not easily adapted to non-Hispanic contexts.

The cathedral of Toledo, as the primatial see of Spain, contains the most abundant records of the organized sacred dancing by boy choirs, but the other Hispanic cathedrals also possessed such customs. Moreover, the repertory of the youths was

---

27. Alfaric and Hoepffner, *La Chanson*, II, 75.

a broad and complex one, yielding insight into the practice as a dramatic form, in which impersonation occurred in varying degrees. Juan Moraleda y Esteban undertook a detailed study of Toledan records on the *seises* and made a strong case for the origins of the well-known Renaissance customs far back in the Visigothic period with which we are dealing. In so doing he looked even further, into the ultimate prototypes of youthful performers in the Biblical accounts of David dancing before the Ark of the Covenant, and the children singing Divine praises at Christ's triumphal entry into Jerusalem before the Passion. Moraleda also recognized the use of boy assistants and servers during the early days of Christianity in the Roman catacombs, under the title of acolytes. All of these remote analogues, however, are presented as dim foreshadowings of the Spanish *mozos de coro* (choir boys) with whose activities he was preoccupied.[28] He asserted that although the boy performers were the norm over the centuries, even into modern times, at some medieval periods their functions at public ceremonies were fulfilled by adults.[29]

The training of children to adorn the liturgy with singing and dancing has been credited by both Moraleda and Simón de la Rosa y López. Ecclesiastical authority recognized the value of leading the minds and hearts of a congregation through the voices and rhythmic gestures of the children, in that the young performers were more innocent and pure in their minds and lives. Their performance would be a pleasing and inspirational form of prayer lifting the affections of the spectators up to God. The prayer would be analogous to that of the angelic choirs praising and blessing the Lord, for indeed these children were accepted as representing the angels in symbolic form.[30]

In theory and in practice this analogy has held the confidence

---

28. Moraleda, *Los Seises*, pp. 10–12, 67–68, 75.

29. Ibid., p. 10.

30. Simón de la Rosa y López, *Los Seises de la Catedral de Sevilla* (Seville: Francisco de P. Díaz, 1904), p. 28; Moraleda, pp. 11–13.

of the Spanish temperament, and ecclesiastical authority was able to safeguard the custom from abuse within the confines of the cathedral structure and to control its implementation. Sacred dance became associated with several great Church feasts, notably Christmas, Corpus Christi (in the late Middle Ages), and the Assumption of Mary (along with other Marian feasts connected with August 15).[31] In my judgment, the firmest testimony that this phenomenon was regarded as sacred and appropriate is the fact that the *seises* danced in the late Middle Ages before the Monstrance in Corpus Christi processions, the presence of the Host in exposition being a most solemn ceremony in Catholic tradition and an extremely sacred occurrence. Rosa y López says that the earliest record at Seville for the dancing of the *seises* at the cathedral is related to Corpus Christi: "'Item pagué á los cantorcillos [i.e., *seises*] que fueron cantando e baylando á la procession del Corpus Christi.'" (Date given as 1508.)[32]

One must admit that the careful regulation of the *mozos de coro* and their later (sixteenth-century) descendants (the *seises*) kept their performances theoretically separate from the popular dance of the parishes and pilgrimage shrines known as *el baile*. Moraleda speaks of the *baile* as a different phenomenon from that of the cathedral boy choristers,[33] but nevertheless the two traditions became in practice intertwined and closely related in many ways. It is this relationship that shows the essential sobriety and sacredness of the dancing at saints' festivals. It also justifies Alfaric's confidence that the popular observances were intended as reverent imitations of the authorized liturgy, even

---

31. Moraleda, p. 17.

32. López, p. 229. Moraleda also gives testimony, pp. 18–19, citing D. Juan Chaves Arcayos' copy (1765) of a manuscript *ordo* from the Toledan cathedral dating from the sixteenth century. The *ordo* refers to the practice as an "antigua costumbre" (p. 182). Moraleda (p. 23) cites also D. Manuel López Coronado, *La Catedral del Toledo y el Ochavo*, a manuscript text with date of 1870, as stating that in earlier centuries the *seises* danced during the Corpus Christi procession.

33. Moraleda, p. 15.

though at times they were occasions of abuse. Moraleda's own research shows this interrelationship to be a fact, and his work dovetails into the views of Ramón Menéndez Pidal on the institution of *juglaría* (the profession of the popular entertainers who were the direct descendants of the Roman *mimi* and the ones generally accepted as public entertainers at saints' festivals). (See Chapter VI, below.)

The term *el baile*, although used to distinguish the folk dancing from the formal choreography of the boy dancers, has a generic meaning that surfaces in the historical discussions in a disconcerting way. Moraleda attempts to keep the two traditions of dance at least logically distinct, but seems to slip into the use of *baile* as simply "dance." In this way he veers from a strict terminological precision, although he attempts to keep on course with periphrastic constructions like *las danzas populares* (p. 62) and *las danzas del pueblo* (p. 15) for the folk performances. From time to time in his pages he uses *baile* and its verb *bailar* as designations for dance in the broadest sense, and even for the performance of the *seises*, as on p. 23, n. 1, where he writes of the children "bailando durante la procesión [of Corpus Christi]." The record from the Seville cathedral, quoted just above, also uses "baylando" in this way.

It is clear that in the later centuries of the Middle Ages and the Renaissance, the popular *baile* had its own public financial supports. Moraleda speaks of payments by municipal authorities for performances of the popular type, that is, payments by "el Municipio" of Toledo and also by craft guilds: "El Municipio también las pagaba, así como los gremios de sederos, pasteleros, guarnicioneros, confiteros y otros" (p. 63). The listing of guilds connected with silk-workers, bakers, jewelers, and confectioners suggests the kind of financial support that the crafts gave to the cycle plays for Corpus Christi in England of the late Middle Ages—a theatrical institution that Spain did not possess.

The *baile*, moreover, was drawn into public ceremonies of ecclesiastical character in these later centuries in a way that testi-
fies to a tradition long known and respected. Moraleda says that
the popular dances were commissioned to adorn the celebrations held to honor a new Cardinal's entrance into his see at
Toledo; and that they were used at official receptions for kings
and princes, as well as to mark great public occasions like the
victory of Lepanto. The audiences for these celebrations were
not restricted, but included archbishops, royalty, notable public
figures, and the people (*pueblo*) in general (pp. 63–64).

Outside of Spain the records of dance as acceptable religious
performance are scattered and late, but they are there. Many of
them have been recorded by Dom L. Gougaud and by E. K.
Chambers but some of the citations need reinterpretation today,
in light of more recent scholarly work. Both of these historians
were concerned with religious dance in general rather than with
the saints' vigils. Gougaud recorded, for example, the organiz-
ing of dance within the churches by the clergy themselves at
Christmastide, including the revelry of January 1, the so-called
Feast of Fools.[34] He also mentions dance interludes in the liturgies of Easter, Ascension, and Pentecost (p. 21). Chambers
records, as does Gougaud, the invasion of church premises
by bands of wanton feminine dancers at high church feasts
throughout the Middle Ages,[35] but these occurrences are the
remnants of pagan tradition not tamed by the Church through
any form of *contrafactum*, and were a recurrent plague in the life
of the parishes. It would be a great mistake, however, to equate
these manifestations with the parish vigil devotions, in the light
of the full story of the sanctoral celebrations.

Reverent religious dance on the day set aside for St. Martial

34. Gougaud, "La Danse dans les églises," *Revue d'histoire ecclésiastique*, 15
(1914), 18–19. See also Dom Gougaud's article on liturgical dance in the *DACL*,
"Danse," Cols. 252–53.
35. Gougaud, "La Danse," pp. 18–19; Chambers; *The Mediaeval Stage*, I, 161.

appears in French records and has survived until our own century at Barjols in Provence.[36] Foatelli has a detailed account of the custom in that town. It was based on a pagan dance occurring when a bull was slain and sacrificed as a way of assuring fertility of the land and success of the growing crops. The Christian customs (from the first centuries) retained the slaying of the ox, with the dance of young men and girls carrying carved slices of the bull to be roasted and sold at a fair. The bull was blessed in the church and the dance of the Tripettes also occurred in the church at the night prayer (Compline) of the Divine Office.[37] The transformation to a Christian ceremony for the feast of St. Marcel or Martial is not very clear, as Foatelli attributes it to an accidental meeting of youths celebrating the pagan fertility rite with Christians searching for the body of St. Marcel buried in an abandoned monastery dedicated to him. The encounter is credited with the origin of the combined dance performance of the Tripettes with honor paid to the Christian saint.

Jacques Chailley recalls the honoring of St. Martial at Limoges, not at the famous abbey bearing the saint's name but at the church of St. Léonard in the town. The record is a thirteenth-century one, and in Chailley's account includes both singing and dancing: "Des danses populaires étaient pratiquées au choeur de Saint Léonard, au XIIIe siècle, et on cite souvent le refrain qui s'y chantait:

Saint Marçau, prega per nos
Et nos espringarem per vos.[38]

Chambers, in referring to this refrain asking St. Martial's prayers in return for the sacred dance in his honor, says that the chant occurred at the end of each psalm in place of "Gloria Pa-

36. Chambers, I, 163.
37. Foatelli, pp. 40–41. Foatelli says it is uncertain whether *Tripettes* refers to the entrails of the ox, or to the pagan dance known as the *tripudium* (associated with augury).
38. Chailley, *L'École musicale de Saint Martial de Limoges* (Paris: Les Livres Essentiels, 1960), p. 372.

tri."[39] This detail points unquestionably to the recitation of the Divine Office and the presence of dance within it.

St. William of Orange, Count of Toulouse and subject of a whole cycle of *chansons de geste,* was a soldier-saint whose shrine was at Gellone, on one of the pilgrimage routes to Compostela.[40] There is a life of this saint by an anonymous author of the eleventh century, who says that he will concentrate on the spiritual side of William's achievements, because his military conquests are well known from public celebrations in his honor.[41] Chambers observes that these celebrations of William's military achievements were folk song of the quasi-epic type.[42] I question this interpretation because the passage here, in its context, clearly indicates chanted hagiography at a Matins office:

Quae enim regna et quae provinciae, quae gentes, quae urbes, Willelmi Ducis potentiam non loquuntur, virtutem animi, corporis vires, gloriosos belli studio et frequentia triumphos? Qui chori juvenum, qui conventus populorum, praecipue militum ac nobilium virorum, quae *vigiliae Sanctorum,* dulce non resonant, et modulatis vocibus decantant, qualis et quantus fuerit. . . .[43] [Emphasis supplied.]

The writer refers specifically to vigils (Matins) for the saint, at which "chori juvenum" perform in his honor, sweetly singing of the saint's greatness, in the presence of a gathering of people that includes military men and the nobility. "Chori" is a word that had had, since classical times, the meaning of song, accompanied by dance, and the "chori juvenum" must here have such significance, comparable to the meaning given to the word in Caesarius' usage.[44]

An illuminating incident occurs in *The Miracles of St. Wulfstan,*

---

39. Chambers, I, 163.

40. Urban Tigner Holmes, *History of Old French Literature,* rev. ed. (New York: Russell and Russell, 1962), pp. 101–02.

41. The *vita* appears in the *Acta Sanctorum* for May 28. See the edition of Carnandet (Paris: V. Palmé, 1866), VI, 801ff.

42. Chambers, I, 27.

43. *Acta,* p. 801.

44. *Oxford Latin Dictionary,* I, 311. Caesarius of Arles had used the word in this sense. See above, Ch. III, n. 71.

in which an indulgent attitude toward a leader of public dance is indicated. It is an account of a performer who became ill ("ciaticus") and, unable to walk, besought St. Wulfstan for a cure. He finally was granted it, as well as a vision of the saint. The minstrel is designated as one of the singers "qui publicos choros ducunt in plateis," and yet he regarded himself as a special servant of St. Wulfstan, ruefully referring to himself as "me peculiarem seruum tuum."[45] The anecdote seems to imply that the *mimus* had led performances of song and dance at the saint's vigil celebrations.

Jacques Chailley has studied the clerical dance at Sens in two of the churches that were dedicated to saints. Starting with references in Du Cange's medieval Latin glossary and in d'Ortigue's *Dictionnaire du Plain-chant,* Chailley went on to search the cathedral records of Sens on the practice of liturgical dance. He found in the choir director's book (MS 6, Bibliothèque Municipale, Sens) that in the thirteenth century the precentor was to dance at the feast of St. Stephen: "'In inventione beati Stephani, ad processionem in navi ecclesiae Senonum precentor debet ballare.'"[46]

Chailley records also the parallel custom of the precentor's annual sacred dance on the feast of St. Loup, who had been an archbishop of Sens. The dance took place at the saint's tomb, in the church of St. Colomba in the city: "'In processione ad sanctam Columbam, precentor in festo sancti Lupi debet ballare.'"[47] The precentor, as choirmaster, here represents an adult fulfillment of the role that in Spain would usually have been performed by the boy *mozos de coro*. Du Cange and d'Ortigue quote

45. *The Miracles of St. Wulfstan,* ed. Reginald Darlington (London: The Royal Society, 1928), p. 135. I am indebted to a graduate student, Martha Oberle, for calling attention to this passage on Wulfstan.

46. Folio 234ᵛ of the manuscript *Precentoris Norma,* as quoted by Chailley, "Un Document nouveau sur la danse ecclésiastique," *Acta Musicologica,* 21 (1949), 20. The "inventione Stephani" probably refers to the discovery of Stephan's tomb in the early fifth century. See above, Chapter IV, pp. 95–96.

47. Chailley, "Un Document," p. 20.

from another source, a chapter statute of Sens directing that the precentor dance at these two churches once a year and at no other time,[48] an indication that the cathedral staff was concerned to keep this phenomenon under careful control.

In summary, then, the official records of councils, episcopal authority, and individual churches reveal that sacred dance was an ambivalent phenomenon, subject to abuse, and eliciting severe condemnations at some times and places, but also permitted, especially in Spain, as a way of expressing religious devotion. Closely associated with the celebration of saints' vigils, it was a transfer of the pagan dance traditions of the Mediterranean world to the Christian observance of festivals dear to the hearts of the people. Serving as a problem for a bishop like Caesarius, this custom was at some times roundly condemned and at others accepted under rather anxious surveillance, but it was to live on into modern times in many places. In order to understand how this ambivalent practice could survive to form the backdrop for medieval drama in the Carolingian era and in the late Middle Ages, it is valuable finally to examine the institution of *juglaría* or *jonglerie* as the tradition of acting that brought together the potential values and perils of an age-old dramatic way of expressing the deepest experiences and emotions of Mediterranean people.

48. Ibid., p. 20.

CHAPTER VI

JUGLARÍA AND THE DRAMATIC
SAINTS' LIVES

The consideration of the saints' lives in Gaul (where recitative dominated) and in Spain (where sacred dance dominated) raises the question whether the performers in these ceremonies were professionals or amateurs. For the High Middle Ages and later centuries there is no problem of documenting a position, but for the Visigothic era the records are sparse and inconclusive. My own position, after years of research and reflection, is that the profession of *juglaría* was the source of the whole undertaking, and that mimic actors and dancers were the ones likely to be drawn upon for the expertise necessary in the project of the *contrafactum*. These events were not ordinary ones but rather the special ceremonies for a famous saint at a cathedral or pilgrimage shrine. Although one cannot easily imagine Caesarius of Arles allowing a *mimus* to perform for him, it is strongly probable that even in these early centuries, the sixth and seventh, the custom of using the professionals was common. Casual allusions to such a practice are so clear and frequent in the twelfth and thirteenth centuries that they bespeak a long tradition behind them that grew out of ancient Mediterranean life. A statement like the one found by Du Méril in the *Romans du Chevalier au cysne* indicates the unquestioned acceptance of the fact: "'La vie saint Morise lor conta uns jogler,'" with the added comment about the audience's eagerness to hear it:

"'Et il furent molt prest d'oïr et escouter.'"[1] Scholarly opinion among the French and Spanish writers has been much more receptive to early prominence of the professional entertainers in the life of the Church than Anglo-American views have been, especially that of E. K. Chambers. It is appropriate to conclude the present study, then, with a consideration of the problem.

In selecting an abstract term to designate the historical phenomenon that is here involved, I have chosen the Spanish word *juglaría* rather than the English "minstrelsy" or the French *jonglerie*. The Spanish term is rich in the denotations of mimicry (the whole range of professional artistry from dance to play-acting) whereas the English one has usually been limited to musical associations, and the French *jonglerie* to connotations of skilled trickery in juggling and slapstick activity. One of the most important contributions to the discussion of *juglaría* was its characterization by Menéndez Pidal as a complex of many professional types of entertainment, with specialization in any one type as the choice of the individual performer.[2] Almost the whole of Part I in his study is an examination of particular terms included under the generic classification of *juglaría*, all of them involving professional entertainment of an audience. If we grasp the complexity of the term, we can appreciate the dangers of generalizing the way of life or the public attitudes experienced by *juglares*. The whole history of public performance in ancient and medieval times is caught up in the Spanish term, as it cannot be contained in any of the other designations, and yet the range of *juglaría* is verifiable throughout the whole of medieval Western Europe.

It was, indeed, an international phenomenon by its origins

1. MS. B. N. Suppl. fr. n° 540^s, fol. 18, v°, col 2, quoted in Édélstand Du Méril, *Les Origines latines*, p. 66.

2. *Poesía juglaresca y juglares*, 6th ed. (Madrid: Espasa-Calpe, S.A., 1969), pp. 11–44. Although my citations are made to this 1969 edition, I have also used the earlier and longer version, *Poesía juglaresca y origines de las literaturas romanicas*, 6th ed. (Madrid: Instituto de Estudios Politicos, 1957).

and its development. At the fall of Rome's great political and social power in the late fifth century, the mimes (as performers) traveled north, encountered the barbarian peoples impinging on their world, and became the entertainers of a new audience that received them gladly: "car ils sont les ancêtres authentiques des jongleurs, et ici, des aïeux aux petits-fils, nous avons tous les intermédiaires. Des plus vieux aux plus jeunes, des carrefours de l'antique Syracuse à ceux des villages de France, ils formeront une chaîne ininterrompue et qui on suit du regard jusqu'au bout."[3] From the public squares of ancient Syracuse (Magna Graecia) to those of French villages—this is the long road traveled by the Graeco-Roman *mimi* as the Empire disappeared and the Germanic tribes invaded the provinces, particularly Gaul.[4]

Much the same general historical analysis of the situation comes from the study of Spanish life in the Middle Ages, as Menéndez Pidal observes that the *juglares* inherited the repertory of the Latin entertainers but recognized the necessity of a gradual and steady adjustment by the performer to the tastes and wishes of his audience: "Aunque el juglar heredó en gran parte *el repertorio de los histriones, mimos y timélicos latinos,* sin duda tenía que transformar continuamente esa herencia. . . ."[5]

Juglaría flourished as a mobile and flexible institution and contact with the Germanic invaders from the north possessing a venerable bardic tradition gave to the Latin performers who encountered them a measure of seriousness and even a social re-

---

3. Faral, *Les Jongleurs,* p. 11. Allardyce Nicoll (pp. 150–68) takes essentially the same stand as Faral on the continuity of the mimic tradition from Graeco-Roman antiquity to the High Middle Ages.

4. On this point, E. K. Chambers had already worked out a theory in which the Latin *mimus* merged his art and repertory with those of the Germanic bard or *Scop,* (I, ch. 2). Faral was adamant in rejecting this notion, insisting that the bard became a *mimus (jongleur),* if he was to survive (pp. 23–24). Menéndez Pidal favored the duality of background (Latin and Germanic) for the *juglares,* and added even a third line of influence for Spain itself, that of Islamic traditions of entertainment from the ninth century (p. 15).

5. Menéndez Pidal, p. 239. (Emphasis supplied.)

spectability that might have eluded them without this confrontation. Professor Chambers exaggerated the famous thesis that he articulated on the fall of the Roman theatre: "The bishops and the barbarians had triumphed."[6] The *mimi* and the *joculatores* were not conquered, as Chambers recorded in his second chapter[7]; rather, they were educated and transformed by the demands of a new era, new audiences, and far-flung pathways.

While one must recognize the enrichment of the jongleur capability through international movement, a student of early medieval history must also give weight to the sovereignty of French fashions over the patterns of creativity and performance in Western Europe. Every civilization attains a superior form in one locale and thus prevails over all participating national expressions of the epoch style. Italy ruled the Europe of the Renaissance and Spain dominated the Baroque era. Medieval culture, then, was French at its core, not only in the High Middle Ages but already in the Romanesque period in which the jongleur tradition was developing. On this point Faral is positive, but cautious in application, limiting himself to the Carolingian era. Under Charlemagne and his immediate successors the jongleurs (so-called from the early ninth century) flourished in France, he says, and by extension in Spain and Italy. France was the leader and innovator in styles of public entertainment as in all other phases of the life and culture of the times.[8]

Faral's observation should be extended and applied to the pre-Carolingian centuries, and I am convinced that his restriction to the ninth and tenth centuries was motivated simply by his caution regarding precise historical documentation in the Visigothic era. He was willing to commit himself to the certainty of Roman mimic traditions in the pre-Carolingian period, but insisted that we cannot be sure just what were their repertory and techniques: "Pendant la période que précède l'âge carolin-

6. Chambers, I, 22.   7. Ibid., pp. 23–41.
8. Faral, p. 17.

gien . . . du moins peut-on affirmer avec certitude qu'ils [i.e.,
the mimes] ont existé et qu'ils ont maintenu toujours vivante la
tradition romaine."[9] Menéndez Pidal has also recognized the
scarcity of documentary evidence in this period of Spanish literature (indeed, in the whole of Spanish life before the twelfth
century),[10] and Muratori has written that in Italy documents are
scarce in all historical matters from the fall of Rome until the
year 1000, and that in the field of public entertainment records
are almost nonexistent.[11] Menéndez Pidal, however, refuses to
accept the scarcity of documented evidence as militating against
the activity of the *juglares* in Spain, and much of his book is a
deduction of evidence for their early importance from later *literary* allusions to them as a long-established institution, and
from allusions by Spanish chroniclers to poems of the *juglares*
no longer extant in our day.[12]

In summary, this position on the origins and nature of the
jongleur tradition accepts the continuity of *juglaría* with the ancient mimic repertory of Graeco-Roman dramatic performance,
and recognizes the international activity of Western European
entertainers in their frequent travels from court to court. This
view finds in the medieval phenomenon a cultural exchange of
great significance, with dominance of the inherited Roman patterns by the innovative, transforming genius of the Gallic spirit.
With this understanding of the mimic tradition, one can pro-

9. Ibid., p. 16. Foatelli (p. 55) also comments on the lack of documentation of
sacred dance for the Visigothic era.
10. Menéndez Pidal, pp. 80–81.
11. Faral cites Muratori without bibliographical detail of any kind here, p. 18,
but the reference is verifiable in Lodovico Muratori, *Antiquitates Italicae Medii
Aevi*, 17 vols. (Arretii: Typis Michaelis Bellotti, 1773–80), II, 831.
12. See, e.g., Menéndez Pidal's discussion on p. 180 and the whole section
pp. 190–218. He also discusses the presence of *mimi* in Spain of the sixth century,
as attested by Gregory of Tours' story of a *mimus regis* healed at the intercession
of St. Martin (*Poesía juglaresca*, pp. 80–81). P. Riché cites casual allusions to
mimic activity in the seventh century, one in the "Vita Amandi," and the other
in the "Vita Praejecti," (Riché, p. 245). The lives of these saints are to be found
in *MGH: Scriptores Rerum Merovingicarum*, ed. B. Krusch and W. Levison, V,
245ff. and 444ff.

ceed to inquire about the attitudes towards these performers in the Mediterranean countries and in the northern European areas affected by their styles of entertainment. This aspect of the question has been a great problem for modern scholarly research, never definitively settled and frequently provoking sharp controversy over apparently irreconcilable theories. The evidence is ambivalent and probably will always remain difficult to interpret. I am convinced that we of the Anglo-American cultural tradition will never fully understand the Latin mind on this institution of *juglaría* (and perhaps on many other similar subjects). Certainly there is no aspect of the medieval drama that has caused a more profound search on my own part and a more thorough revision of judgment during years of study and reflection.

The range of medieval attitudes towards *juglaría* is a very broad one, from the ancient Roman stigma of *infamia* placed upon all actors to the respectful imitation of *joculatores* by medieval friars in the Franciscan tradition. There is ambivalence and even contradiction in these Continental records, and one comes to agree with Menéndez Pidal that the *juglares* were throughout their history, from Roman antiquity and the Patristic era and even into their thirteenth century of splendor, "seres contradictorios, medio ángeles, medio diablos."[13] Their origins were ultimately pagan, their repertory often contained scurrilous buffoonery, and they were capable of distracting the Christian faithful from devout celebration of religious festivals. Nevertheless, they were a solace for weary or broken spirits and were a vital educational and cultural force, and they often narrated edifying stories of heroic warriors and saints. Contradictory beings, indeed, they were.

Let us consider the basic negative attitudes. The Latin countries never freed themselves completely from the ancient legal stance that members of the acting profession were outside the

13. *Poesía juglaresca,* p. 61.

pale of Roman citizenship. *Mimi* and *histriones* normally were, or had been, slaves, and were excluded from the juridical rights of voting, pleading in the law courts, and holding equestrian or senatorial rank.[14] This stigma excluding them from major civil rights had the technical name of *infamia*, and constituted a caste system of considerable rigidity.[15] The formal position as given in the *Corpus Juris Civilis* includes both the actors of the legitimate theater and those who performed by reading and recitation in the mimic and pantomimic repertory.[16] Chambers discusses the continued duration of this statutory regulation through the centuries of the Empire, with only minor variations and relaxations of severity, for example, under Theodosius;[17] and he records a late Carolingian decree imposing *infamia* upon entertainers of various kinds.[18] Menéndez Pidal finds that even as late as the thirteenth century in Spain the legal code connected with Alfonso of Castile's reign and known as the *Siete Partidas* repeats strictures against *juglares* that are essentially those of the Roman statutory *infamia;* ancient law and social attitudes are being repeated without bringing them into harmony with the contemporary conditions of thirteenth-century Castile or even the favorable observations about entertainers contained elsewhere in the code.[19]

The second cause of hostility to the *mimi* is that of moral turpitude in their repertory, and even in ancient Rome this charge was made by both political and ethical thinkers. Any historical account of the Graeco-Roman comedy as realized in these per-

14. Chambers details this historical foundation of civic hostility to the acting profession (I, 8–10, 38–39).

15. The attitude is older than Roman society and probably is related to Greek exclusion of performing arts from the life of the free man; but this story is outside the scope of the present work.

16. Chambers (I, 8) quotes an extract from the *Digest* that brands with *infamia* anyone who appeared on stage as actor or reciter ("'artis ludicrae pronuntiandive causa in scaenam prodierit'").

17. Ibid., pp. 9–22.

18. Ibid., p. 38.

19. Menéndez Pidal, pp. 61–62.

formers adverts to their reputation for indecency and scurril-
ity.[20] The same charge is frequently made also of the legitimate
comic stage, in the works of Plautus and Terence, however fine
the Latin style of their composition. The Mediterranean comic
spirit has always been judged as coarse and robust by northern
Europeans, and mimic theater often did descend to the lowest
level of boisterous immorality. Chambers draws a vivid picture
of the pagan emperor, Marcus Aurelius, sitting in the imperial
box at the circus and reading a philosophical text instead of
watching a performance of the mimes.[21] This pose of the emperor was a public show of disapproval for the decadent comic
art prevailing on the Roman stage in his day, but it is also a
symbol of the political expediency that continued to give the
populace its bread and circuses whatever the ethical price to be
exacted. Allardyce Nicoll concedes the presence of obscenity in
the mimic repertory, but calls attention to the serious philosophical observations made by responsible Romans familiar with the
mimes. Cicero, Seneca, and Petronius expressed admiration for
the thoughtful wisdom embedded in the poetic lines of the
mimic scripts, especially in the work of Publilius Syrus.[22] The
substance of these compositions reflected the whole range of
human life, and was not limited to the pornography that was
directed at vulgar audiences (p. 127). "The mime in essence was
the very incarnation, the first ideal of that *mimesis* on which is
based the whole of the peripatetic literary theory . . ." (p. 82),
and Nicoll speaks for the genuine artistry that frequently transcended the swaggering farce.

The Christian moral theologians of the Patristic Age were frequent critics of the late Roman theater. Here again Chambers
surveys the field with meticulous care but the impression one
gets is that the pastoral problem was more complex than the

20. See, e.g., Allardyce Nicoll's Chapter II, "The Heyday of Mimic Drama,"
especially pp. 115–27.
21. Chambers, I, 10.
22. Nicoll, p. 115.

denunciation of obscenity. A converted Augustine certaintly denounced the corrupt theater, even of the serious tragic type, and scorned the mimic performance as much below the literary drama, and more dangerous to a Christian's morality.[23] The Fathers of the Church seemed concerned, however, with dangers to the faith of the early Christians from the theater as much as with their problems of morality. The drama was used in the conflict between Christian and pagan religious life as a whole, and comic mockery of the new faith was part of that struggle. Sermons of denunciation refer to the theater as a rival of the Church liturgy in holy seasons and festivals. Christians were not forbidden attendance at the plays and mimes in an absolute sense, but were restricted in patronage of them on Sundays and holy days.[24] The condemnations and the opposition vary under particular circumstances (for example, for the laity as distinguished from clergy). The problem of the theater in the Patristic Age was a part of the much larger difficulty of determining the Christian's relationship to the whole pagan culture of the ancient world, with its philosophy, literature, and religious worship.[25] The morality or immorality of the theater was a part of the issue, and must have been solved in varying ways for the practicing Christians of the day, except in extremely rigorous approaches like that of Tertullian.

Christine Schnusenberg has recently surveyed again the whole problem of Patristic antagonism to the Roman theater and has supported the basically religious rather than moral foundation of this antagonism. The Church Fathers saw in the theater an educational and cultural force closely allied to Roman religion, and recognized that state religious festivals were often marked by performances of plays. As the Church developed its

23. *De Civitate Dei*, II, 8 as discussed by Chambers, I, 17–18.
24. Chambers, I, 11–22.
25. See Pierre de Labriolle, *Histoire de la littérature latine chrétienne*, 3rd ed., 2 vols. (Paris: Les Belles-Lettres, 1947). The first chapter of Volume I surveys this complex problem of the early Church's orientation to Graeco-Roman pagan culture.

own liturgy, it fostered a rival sense of "congregation" competing with the pagan one, but gradually imitated some of the Roman techniques in its own structure of liturgical worship.[26] Schnusenberg's study, however, is not a theatrical one. There is little allusion to actual plays or to modes of performance. Her interest is in modes of expression, above all, in allegory and symbolism, that may be designated by the adjective "dramatic" but that seem to defeat the very nature of drama as structured imitation of action. Her work, however, is valuable in locating the hostility of the Church leaders towards the theater on theological rather than ethical grounds.[27]

In medieval, as distinct from ancient, attacks on the morality of the *joculatores*, one class or type of entertainer receives special exemption from the condemnations. This is the narrative raconteur, and the singling out of such a group reveals a marked partiality toward the teller of tales. He is sequestered from the *jongleur*, who is the singer of courtly amorous lyrical compositions coming from the creative artistry of the troubadours. The respect accorded to the narrative as opposed to the lyrical performer is based on the positive and beneficent effect of the great stories when chanted or read to an audience fascinated by heroic characters and virtuous deeds. The distinction is a fundamental one and is not simply a grudging concession to a small number of exceptionally virtuous entertainers. The class singled out in this way was a major component of the numerous progeny descended from the ancient *mimi*, and it helped to rescue from scorn and censure the profession of *juglaría* as such. Menéndez says that although a *juglar* could become proficient in both narrative and lyrical materials, the records do not show that he customarily did so. He was a specialist in one type.[28]

The approval and good will shown to narrative recitation are

---

26. Schnusenberg, *Das Verhältnis von Kirche und Theater* (Bern: Peter Lang, 1981). Her general view is worked out in pp. 1–60.

27. See her consideration of Augustine's outlook, pp. 37–39.

28. *Poesía juglaresca*, p. 35.

well known in medieval studies as they appeared in the phrasing of Thomas de Cabham's *Penitential,* but they have been narrowly interpreted as an insignificant indulgence to a few pious entertainers. Cabham's famous dictum expressed a positive attitude toward "'joculatores qui cantant gesta principum et vitas sanctorum,'"[29] while condemning other kinds of entertainers, notably singers of amorous lyrics and satirical compositions. Chambers' handling of this material in Cabham's *Penitential* seems considerably less satisfactory than Faral's. The French scholar recognizes this thirteenth-century formulation by the Sub-Dean of Salisbury Cathedral as the normal and general ecclesiastical position throughout the Middle Ages, precisely codified in that century distinguished by precise formulations and academic analysis (of moral and dogmatic problems). Cabham himself referred to Pope Alexander for a similar toleration of the *joculatores* who confined their repertory to the heroic and hagiographical stories (probably Alexander III).[30] Thomas Aquinas, writing in the same century, excluded from sinfulness all entertainers whose materials were good in themselves, without specifying the genre of the recitations or performances. Aquinas and Cabham are at one in expressing ecclesiastical permission for wholesome play and recreation, St. Thomas giving the general philosophical principle and Cabham the practical application to existing repertories.[31]

Faral recognizes that the two types of narratives singled out by the *Penitential* are the *chansons de geste* ("gesta principum") and the saints' legends ("vitas sanctorum"). He considers these two kinds of edifying story to be so closely related as almost to form a single genre, and to be characterized by the same literary

29. Faral, p. 44. Chambers quotes the *Penitential,* in his second volume of the *Mediaeval Stage,* Appendix G, and discusses it in I, 59–62.

30. Chambers, I, 59 n. 2.

31. Chambers quotes Thomas' view from the *Summa Theologiae,* II, 2, quaest. 168, art. 3. Menéndez Pidal, p. 63, observes that moral theologians made more careful distinctions in this problem than did the contemporary compilers of legal codes.

style.[32] He is, quite clearly, referring to vernacular narratives, including such stories from the tenth century up to the late Middle Ages. What he says, however, is of immense importance for the role that saints' lives played in the repertory of the medieval entertainers from the very beginning, and should clarify the place of the Gallican saints' *vitae* in the pre-Carolingian age. The whole point of reassessing the institution of *juglaría*, as I see it, is to throw into relief the close association of popular entertainment in the mimic tradition with the pastoral work of the Church, already in the Visigothic and Gallican centuries (sixth to eighth). *Juglaría* was an educational force, available and actually employed, for the spiritual cultivation of semi-barbaric Christians still speaking Latin, and capable of being taught both by churchmen and by professional entertainers in that language.

The positive and favorable attitudes toward *juglaría* can thus emerge into a stronger light and take their proper place in the total historical picture of medieval life. Defense of the *juglar* or *jongleur* was not a *tour de force* of libertine opinion, but was the theologian's thoughtful recognition of the human need for wholesome relaxation; a recognition also of the potential refinement that the human spirit can undergo in attending to the great heroic legends professionally told. Menéndez Pidal names several Spanish rulers who developed a philosophical position quite strongly supportive of *juglaría*, regarding the role of professional entertainment as indispensable in a well-ordered life: "San Fernando, Alfonso el Sabio, Jaime II de Mallorca o Pedro IV de Aragón los [juglares] llegan a juzgar indispensables para una vida ordenada."[33]

Official recognition of the *juglares* as necessary adjuncts to a royal household was based on the positive contribution they made to the normal operation of governmental functions.

32. Faral, pp. 46–48.
33. Menéndez Pidal, p. 61.

Thomas de Cabham himself had included in his favorable estimate of the *joculatores* discussed above that those who properly
narrated the heroic and saintly stories gave relief to human
cares and infirmities.[34] Testimony to the healing efficacy of the
singer, instrumentalist, and dancer is abundant in records of the
High Middle Ages, both of the statutory and literary kind. The
ruler of a country, as well as his retinue of councilors and retain-
ers, experienced the heavy weight of pervasive governmental
duties and problems. Relief from these burdens was legiti-
mately sought in the delightful refreshment accorded by the
musical beauty of a singer's voice or of his *vihuela*. The *juglar*
took his place at the table or in the great hall of the castle, ad-
justing his performance to the needs of the occasion, whether
for merriment, relaxation, or consolation.[35] The household regulations of Jaime II contained the admission that *juglares* participated in the effective governing activity of the realm by soft-
ening the heart of the king and easing his tensions in the midst
of harassing problems.

The *jongleur* had his respected place also at the bedside of the
sick, so that the ministrations of a physician could be supplemented by the resources of the entertainers. Here it is not
simply a case of distraction from physical pain, although that
kind of relief was sought for the ill and the wounded. The *juglar*
was a trusted and valued anodyne also for mental illness (if that
term is not too much steeped in modern *angst*). His recitation
and the musical accompaniment that he could provide brought
consolation in personal grief and could root out the sorrow of
unrequited love or the paralyzing torpor of melancholy depres-
sion. This kind of reliance upon the healing power of the performing artist is attested not only in literary accounts like the
story of Appolonius, but also in the life records of actual per-

34. Ibid., p. 63.
35. Ibid., p. 45.

sons like Álvaro de Luna and Juan Hurtado de Mendoza, to whom such quasi-medical care was recommended by friends.[36]

The singer of tales was also a participant in the glorification of his country's historical greatness. Although he was usually the performer rather than the composer of narratives, he nevertheless served to propagate and preserve a kind of popular history upon which the learned chroniclers later drew. The *juglares* had an educative role ("una misión de enseñanza histórica"),[37] and were "colaboradores en la historia y mantenedores del sentimiento nacional" (p. 206). A whole section of Menéndez Pidal's *Poesía juglaresca* (pp. 169–237) is largely devoted to the task of demonstrating that late medieval Spanish chroniclers drew upon the much earlier and more popular historical accounts circulating among the *juglares*, who thus preserved the facts and legends of heroism for generations to come. Moreover, he expresses the opinion that this educational function of the narrative reciters was fundamental to the ecclesiastical approbation of their activity and to their escape from the excommunication imposed upon most of the other professional entertainers (p. 171). To this glorification of past magnificence and bravery should be added the persuasive rhetorical powers of the *jongleur* in leading men to battle for the defense of country or in crusade for the Faith. The role of the military poet in the retinue of the medieval champion is so old and so pervasive that it cannot be attributed simply to the tradition of Latin *joculatores*, but it formed a part of the bardic responsibility in European life and certainly entered into the respect and favor shown by kings and noblemen for their minstrel attendants on the battlefield.[38]

36. Ibid., pp. 60–61. Glending Olsen, although not dealing with *juglaría* or the drama, has some valuable general observations on medieval medical conceptions of good health as supported by the pleasures of recreational reading. (*Literature as Recreation in the Middle Ages* [Ithaca: Cornell University Press, 1982], pp. 39–63.)

37. Menéndez Pidal, p. 171.

38. Chambers, I, 43–44; Menéndez Pidal, pp. 59–60.

Finally, the *juglares* were directly in the service of the Church and were patronized by monasteries and the houses of ecclesiastical prelates. Nothing is more puzzling to the modern reader than this fact, and it needs careful examination for an understanding of its significance. Early records are not easily available on the matter. The testimony for ecclesiastical patronage is, however, abundant in the centuries from the twelfth to the fifteenth and serves as a sign of long-established custom, built up not by precept or law but by the *mores* of a society constructed on the foundations of the Roman Empire. Here Chambers' materials are quite misleading and are genuinely in need of reassessment, as O. B. Hardison pointed out a few years ago.[39]

Menéndez Pidal emphasizes again and again that the *juglares* were called upon to participate in church festivals of all kinds, as a regular feature of the celebrations. Their musical ability and their professional skills in reading or narrating to an audience made them immensely valuable adjuncts of the clergy in the direction of ecclesiastical events. The clerical writer often fulfilled the role of composer, translating or adapting a saint's life, for example, in the vernacular speech; but his compositions were meant for recitation or performance by a *juglar*. The collaboration of the clerical author, trained in hagiography and theology, was given to his professional colleague, who was skilled in the performing arts.[40] It was a flourishing partnership and it was the normal way of managing the decorous observation of a great church festival.

A series of articles by the Benedictine scholar, Dom Jean Le-

39. Chambers, I, Chapter 2, pp. 23–41; Chapter 3, pp. 42–62. Professor Hardison offers a critique of Chambers' whole study, the *Mediaeval Stage*, in the introductory chapter of *Christian Rite and Christian Drama in the Middle Ages*, pp. 5–18, but he is preoccupied with Chambers' relationship to historical methodology and the theory of evolution in literary forms. Dr. Hardison does point out in the British scholar a bias against Christianity, and an anticlericalism that portrays the medieval ecclesiastics as constantly at war with the mimetic instincts of the folk (pp. 14–17).

40. Menéndez Pidal, pp. 58–59.

clercq,[41] has reopened the problem of *juglaría* in the Church, and his view was subsequently challenged by an Italian writer. Father Leclercq studied closely the knowledge that St. Bernard of Clairvaux had of *juglaría* and his attitude towards it. The twelfth-century Cistercian ascetic reveals a wide and deep awareness of the phenomenon and a genuine acceptance of the positive values in the jongleur's approach to the world. The overthrow of secular values by a carelessness towards them seems to emerge from the performer's wandering ways and his comic sense about life. His profession could thus be seen as a powerful weapon for the enrichment of monastic spirituality,[42] analogous to the Franciscan apostolate to the laity using the array of dramatic and narrative techniques for pastoral teaching purposes.

Chiara Frugoni responded to Dom Jean's essays with a fundamental denial of ecclesiastical openness to the jongleuristic profession.[43] Stating absolutely that the Church has always deeply opposed music, dance, and song as pagan, sensual, and worldly, she insisted that favorable analyses of *juglaría* were only metaphorical and illustrative, without admitting any genuine spiritual values in the way of life itself.[44] Much of her essay resembles the attitudes already expressed by Chambers, and her challenge to Dom Leclercq's estimate of the phenomenon seems superficial. One point that both scholars make is that many *juglares* were themselves clerics in the High Middle Ages, and therefore trained singers, who valued the clerical tonsure because it gave them a secure and wide acceptance in their trav-

41. Leclercq, "Le Thème de la jonglerie chez St. Bernard et ses contemporains," *Revue d'histoire de la spiritualité*, 48 (1972), 385–400; "Joculator et Saltator: S. Bernard et l'image du jongleur dans les manuscrits," in *Translatio Studii: Honoring O. L. Kapsner* (Collegeville, Minn.: St. John's University Press, 1973), pp. 124–48.
42. Leclercq, "Le Thème," passim.
43. C. Frugoni, "La Rappresentazione dei giullari nelle chiese fino al XII sec.," in *Il Contributo dei giullari* (Viterbo: Centro di Studi sul Teatro Mediovale e Rinascimentale, 1977), pp. 124–27.
44. Ibid., pp. 115–16.

els.[45] With this admission, it seems to me, the whole case against *juglaría* really collapses and its availability as a normal instrument of ecclesiastical life is confirmed.

The Spanish study (*Poesía juglaresca*) makes its greatest contribution to the understanding of European minstrelsy at precisely this point. Menéndez Pidal insisted that his position was one that confronted a formidable array of medieval scholars working in the field before him.[46] He chose as his most distinguished exemplar of the clerical poet writing for the *juglar* the thirteenth century Gonzalo de Berceo, who wrote a verse life of San Millán for the pilgrimage throngs that gathered at the monasteries of Santo Domingo (Silos) and San Millán de la Cogolla. This poet thought of himself as "juglar de cosas espirituales" and addressed himself to the saint as a devotee, entitled to be called "tu juglar."[47] Berceo gives life and reality to the famous metaphor used by Francis of Assisi when he spoke of his new order as made up of *joculatores Domini*. Nothing is more striking than the idea that emerges clearly from Menéndez Pidal's study: that the Franciscans were not using a figure of speech, were not ascribing a metaphorical dimension to their apostolate, but were literally *joculatores* of spiritual life, using the whole panoply of song, musical accompaniment, and recitation directly in the service of pastoral work.[48] This attribution of spiritual function to the professional minstrel is not only a triumph of the performing art in difficult surroundings, but it is a testimony to the great need for the modern scholar to see the medieval phenomenon of *juglaría* in its own historical context—a pagan Roman tradition gradually transformed into a Christian instrument—for the joy and solace of the people gathered in the public square or at the sacred shrine.

The present chapter has been an attempt to draw out and em-

45. Leclercq, "Joculator et Saltator," p. 131; Frugoni, p. 123.
46. Menéndez Pidal, p. 194.
47. Ibid., p. 192.
48. Wardropper, *Historia de la poesín lirica*, pp. 9–10, also takes this view.

phasize the case that has been made for an unbroken continuity between the ancient Roman mimic tradition of dramatic performance and the repertory of medieval *juglaría*. Such a continuity reveals a controversial duality in the cultural significance of medieval entertainers. It reveals the *jongleurs* as "contradictory beings," steeped in the legal and social *infamia* of ancient Rome but nevertheless capable of transformation in a Christian society into a respected class of skilled ministers to the joy and spiritual well-being of their patrons. In the task of reassessment, the work of Edmond Faral and Menéndez Pidal has been the basic resource, and the comparison of their positions with those of E. K. Chambers has led to suggestions of revision and adjustment of the British scholar's viewpoints, notably his bias against the medieval clergy as censors of the mimetic instinct.

CONCLUSION

As we look back over the Visigothic era, we find Caesarius of Arles as the most significant figure for the history of medieval dramatic origins and for the development of the Gallic liturgies. His name appears again and again in the present study and calls for a final estimate. Although he was a stern opponent of the abuses discussed above, his influence must not be evaluated in a purely negative sense. He denounced the pagan character of mime and dance in thunderous sermons, it is true, but he also encouraged the reverent observance of the martyrs' festivals in a very creative way, different from that of public reading at a sacred shrine, fulfilling the principle of the *contrafactum* in a shrewd and persuasive manner. His denunciations witness to the continuity of pagan dramatic customs well into the sixth century, and yet his positive programs were built into the known structures of the saints' vigils. He created out of the chaos following the collapse of the Roman Empire a viable way of Christian life and spirituality for both the Gallic survivors of the Mediterranean world and the newly converted peoples who had moved from the Germanic lands of the north. He was a most effective agent in developing aspects of the Gallican liturgy in southern France and introduced observances like the recitation of the "Little Hours" in the Divine Office, which created a structure of prayer life for the laity as well as for the poorly educated clergy in a bewildering age. Since his sermons were copied and widely distributed, he continued to be influential long after his death and far beyond the limits of Gallican spirituality.

His program for the instruction of his people was quite truly a plan for raising an illiterate constituency to a level comparable to the Gallo-Roman culture in the last years of the Empire. Knowing, of course, that most of his people could not read, and yet desiring to immerse them in Biblical wisdom, he urged the few who were literate to read Scripture, and those who were not, to listen as others read it aloud. His practical suggestion for the logistics of this program was a division of labor in which those who could do the reading would be compensated financially by those who listened. He drew a parallel with merchants who paid secretaries and accountants to do the paper work for which they themselves were not equipped. In Sermon 8, "On Perseverance in Reading," he observed that some wealthy people are illiterate and some learned ones are poor. Why not use this opportunity, he asked, so that the rich man paid a wage to the poor man for the labor of reading in the household? This practice would create a viable exchange of goods in a truly pedagogical undertaking. His expectations of his people are staggering, as he urges them (Sermons 6 and 7) to read or listen to Scripture in the long evenings of the winter for a period of three hours! He also urged that the lay people have discussion groups after a sermon heard in the church, each one bringing a few thoughts from the homily and contributing them to the pool of ideas, so that the total sermon would be reconstructed, discussed among them, and eventually followed in practice within their individual lives (Sermon 6).

Against a background of such religious education for the laity, Caesarius' care for the training of his clergy was complementary. He insisted on the obligation of preaching that he expected both of bishops and priests, and he undertook the task of supplying them with homiletic material for public reading. In his cathedral school of St. Stephen at Arles, he set up a scriptorium in which seminarians studying for the priesthood made copies of sermons to be distributed among the bishops under his jurisdiction. These would often be homilies of the early Church Fathers, especially of St. Augustine, to which Caesarius would add prefaces and conclusions and sometimes passages of his own composition.[1] These collections of sermons were multiplied far beyond the diocese of Arles and its subordinates, becoming well known in Spain and England, and in missionary territories of the Germanic people, used, for example, by Boniface in his evangelizing work.[2]

In such pedagogical endeavors, the dominance of reading or listening is clearly discernible, and Caesarius rested his program solidly on it. Consequently, the reading of saints' lections at the public hagiographical celebrations falls into proper perspective as part of this total design, and it is not surprising that he should make no concessions to dance or song as a *contrafactum* in transforming the vigil festivals. Caesarius' horror of the pagan mimic traditions, as outlined above, could accept no compromise with the abuses he found among the people in attendance. He made no attempt to abolish the cherished vigil celebrations, but he urged for them a spirit of piety, devotion, and genuine asceticism.

His most important admonitions occur in Sermons 223, 224, and 225, all "On Feasts of Holy Martyrs." Dom Morin has indicated that these are Caesarius' own work, not centos or *florilegia*.[3] Each one of the three concentrates on a single theme with a practical application of it. In 223, he exhorts those coming to the vigil that they imitate the self-abnegation of the martyrs, not by physical death but by the conquest of vices like drunkenness, and by forgiveness of enemies. In 224, the theme is preparation for the saint's festival by repentance and almsgiving. The third exhortation is a plea for genuine holiness, based on the spiritual

1. Sister M. M. Mueller discusses this program of Caesarius in the Introduction to her translation (pp. xx–xxiii) and cites the article of Dom Morin in which he details the complicated task that ensued for him in making a critical edition, designating the passages that are Caesarius' own and identifying the authorship of the traditional material in which the inserted paragraphs are embedded. (Dom Morin's article, "The Homilies of St. Caesarius of Arles," appears in *Orate Fratres*, 14 [1939–40], 481–86.)
2. Mueller, pp. xxii–xxiii.
3. Morin, *Sermones*, prefatory notes to Nos. 223, 224, 225.

conquests that result from frequenting the same Sacraments as the martyrs did, serving as soldiers fighting spiritual battles under the same King and Leader. This is the sermon that he concludes by urging his conscientious people to dissuade and even rebuke those who are marking the saint's festival with such abuses as "saltare, choros ducere, verba turpia proferre."[4]

Caesarius, then, labored to transform the saint's vigil festivities not by adapting the mimic techniques of Roman drama to Christian worship but by directly transforming the hearts and wills of the people themselves through his sermon rhetoric and their reading. The principle of the *contrafactum* is here being applied in the spirit of Augustine, who had urged allegorizing the acts of singing and dancing at vigils into religious teachings by the clergy, on the one hand, and on the other, devout performance of virtuous deeds by the congregation.[5] This method was not the only way of purifying the *mores* of a people, as the history of the Visigothic era reveals. The Spanish religious context, and even that of some churches in Gaul, was more propitious to the retention of recitative and mimic dance themselves, while disciplining them to the service of lay spirituality. As Prosper Alfaric commented, the mixed nature of the vigil service, containing pagan and Christian conditions, reveals why the pastoral methods of transformation should differ according to local customs and to the personal temperament of a bishop like Caesarius.

A quarter of a century ago Hardin Craig observed that the saints' plays of the late Middle Ages seemed to have no discernible origins in Latin liturgy comparable to the plays of Christmas and Easter found all over Western Europe from the Carolingian Age onwards. He expressed the opinion, however, that the puzzle of the saints' compositional history as drama might one day be solved in liturgical terms similar to those of the other

4. Caesarius, II, 891.
5. See above, Chapter III, n. 40 for Augustine's exhortation in Sermon cccxi.

genres.[6] The present study has been an attempt to solve that riddle in a paraliturgical manner, by offering the public recitation of saints' lives, accompanied by mimic gesture, as a history of hagiographical drama in the early medieval centuries. The phenomenon was a special educational project in the chaotic cultural conditions following the collapse of the Roman Empire, covering the centuries from the sixth to the tenth—a period long regarded by historians as a dark and silent age: the darkness of barbarian invasion and widespread illiteracy, and the silence of a world without texts and without a theater. Even those historians like Bonilla y San Martin, who were firmly convinced that Roman drama never died out but was maintained as a continuous heritage in the Mediterranean area, quailed before the task of finding a dramatic tradition actually operative in the Christian culture of the age following the Empire.

The supposition that saints' lives read aloud in a professional manner constituted this tradition and that it was a form of dramatic impersonation supplies a chain of continuity between a pagan, secular theater and the religious, monastic drama of the tenth century. Three forms of realization are here involved in the Gallican and Hispanic *vitae:* (1) a public recitative at a shrine, accompanied at least occasionally by music and dance; (2) private group-readings in the households of the affluent, who could compensate educated readers for serving as instruments for the sanctoral stories, appealing to a barely educated Christian people in a barbaric age; (3) a tradition of sacred dance as central to the theatrical presentation by boy choristers and child actors in a specifically Spanish paradigm.

The suppression of the Gallican liturgy by the Frankish rulers beginning in the mid-eighth century has been itself an equivocal event in the history of drama. Karl Young wondered why a linguistic purification of decadent Latin texts, aiming at a Classical

6. Craig, *English Religious Drama of the Middle Ages* (London: Oxford University Press, 1955), pp. 83, 323.

vocabulary and syntax, should have flowered into a troping movement of exotic lyrical beauty and terminated in a monastic drama.[7] Cyrille Vogel suggested that the suppression of the Gallican liturgy was aimed at severing the heavy Byzantine influence, with its allegorical modes of theological expression, that had developed in the Gallican texts.[8] These are unsolved puzzles and theories, to which one might add that the suppression was really a strike against the saints' lives dominating the devotional life of southern Gaul; the suppression was a Roman administrative move to discourage the exotic, provincial, and rather primitive lections still being read at Matins and Mass in the eighth century.

That the Gallican and Hispanic practices were tenacious, however, the well-known ceremonies honoring St. Fides (Foy) reveal as late as the eleventh century. The text of her *vita* makes allusion to the fact that it was a mimed Spanish song translated into French for the pilgrims flocking to her shrine at Conques.[9] Bernard of Angers has left a detailed account of his own visit to Conques and of a miracle that occurred when the pilgrims were temporarily excluded from the night vigil in honor of St. Foy.[10] The recitative given to her life was a late survival of the dramatic tradition that the two territories had fostered for centuries.

Another form of the practice became popular in the late eleventh and twelfth centuries as a substitute for the public reading. G. Raynouard records that the suppression of the Gallican rite included a prohibition against reading of any non-Scriptural lection in the Mass.[11] This regulation was a direct blow at the saints' lives, the vast majority of which were hagiographical

---

7. Young, I, 180–82.
8. Vogel, "Le Développement historique du culte chrétien en occident," *Problemi di storia della Chiesa: l' Alto Medioevo* (Milan: Vita e Pensiero, 1973), II, 93–94.
9. *La Chanson de sainte Foy de Conques*, ed. and trans. Augustin Fabre (Rodez: Éditions de la Revue Historique de Rouergue, 1940), p. 3.
10. Bernard d'Angers, *Liber Miraculorum Sancte Fidis*, ed. A. Bouillet (Paris: Picard, 1897), II, 120–22.
11. Raynouard, II, cxlvii–viii.

compositions of a popular nature. The so-called farced epistle was a Scriptural lesson of a general character, into which a particular saint's life could be inserted in short phrases filling out the authentic Scriptural passage. A selection appropriate for a generic type, for example a martyr-bishop, could be given these fragmentary expansions so as to suggest the outline of a particular life, like that of St. Clement. It became customary to have one clerical voice chant the Scriptural passage and another one to add the "farced," that is, troped, material. This practice was widespread in France throughout the High Middle Ages, and also in England and Spain, and needs a separate study in itself.[12] Quantitatively, the farced lections for St. Stephen's feast dominate the genre, and his day within the Christmas octave became the focus of many dramatic customs reminiscent of the proscribed Gallican practices of earlier centuries. F. J. Fétis indicates that the composition and chanting of farced epistles were permitted by the French bishops in recognition of the popular disappointment over the loss of participation in the Gallican liturgy, long known and cherished by them.[13]

The end product of this heritage was the saint's play of the twelfth century, the genre represented by the St. Nicholas Latin dramas in France and Germany and by many vernacular miracle plays in French of the late Middle Ages. The genre flourished in England,[14] but most of the texts have been lost, most prob-

12. This research, in which I have long been interested, must begin with a study of Clemens Blume's edition of farced epistles in *Analecta Hymnica Medii Aevi* (Leipzig: O. R. Reisland, 1906), Vol. 49. See my article, "The Origin of the Middle English Saints' Plays," in *The Medieval Drama and its Claudelian Revival*, ed. C. Dunn, T. Fotitch, and B. Peebles (Washington: The Catholic University of America Press, 1970), pp. 1–15.

13. F. J. Fétis, *Histoire générale de la musique*, V, 106–7. On the relationship of the Gallican and Roman liturgies in the Carolingian era, as distinguished from the earlier period, see Clifford Flanigan's essay, "The Roman Rite and the Origins of the Liturgical Drama."

14. See the recent collection of essays edited by Clifford Davidson, *The Saint Play in Medieval Europe* (Western Michigan University: Medieval Institute Publications, 1986), in which the essay on the Middle English saints' plays is by Davidson and the one on the French plays by Lynette R. Muir.

ably destroyed during the conflicts of the Reformation struggle, in which hagiographical devotion suffered widespread attacks. Records of many English plays, without surviving texts, prove the popularity of the type well into the sixteenth century.[15] The vicissitudes of the genre were many and the various attempts to acclimate a sanctoral narrative in changing cultural conditions lead back to the earliest form of medieval religious drama—as I see it—the public recitations of the Gallican liturgy in the sixth and seventh centuries, adamant in survival under changing forms for a thousand years.

15. Craig, pp. 320–34.

SELECT BIBLIOGRAPHY

Abrams, Meyer. *The Mirror and the Lamp: Romantic Theory and the Critical Tradition.* New York: W. W. Norton, 1958.

Acta Sanctorum. Ed. Joannes Carnandet. Paris: V. Palmé, 1863ff.

Aigrain, René. *L'Hagiographie: Ses sources, ses méthodes, son histoire.* Paris: Bloud & Gay, 1953.

Alessandro, Silvio. Letter to the author, 16 June 1987.

Alfaric, Prosper, and Ernest Hoepffner. Eds. *La Chanson de Sainte Foy.* 2 vols. Strasbourg: Publications françaises de l'université de Strasbourg, 1926; London: Oxford University Press, 1928.

Analecta Hymnica Medii Aevi. Ed. Clemens Blume. Leipzig: O. R. Reisland, 1905–6. (*Tropi Graduales,* Vol. 49.)

Andrieu, Michel. *Les 'Ordines Romani' du haut moyen âge.* 5 vols. Louvain: "Spicilegium sacrum lovaniense," Bureaux, 1931–61.

Anglès, Higini. *La Musica a catalunya fins al segle XIII.* Barcelona: Institut d'estudis catalans, 1935.

————. "Latin Chant before St. Gregory." *The New Oxford History of Music.* London: Oxford University Press, 1955. Vol. 2.

Aston, S. C. "The Saint in Medieval Literature." *MLR,* 65 (1970), xxv–xlii.

Aubé, Benjamin. *Polyeucte dans l'histoire.* Paris: Firmin-Didot, 1882.

Auerbach, Erich. *Literary Language and its Public in Late Latin Antiquity and in the Middle Ages.* Trans. Ralph Manheim. Bollingen Series LXXIV. New York: Pantheon Books, 1965.

Augustine of Hippo. *Epistulae. Corpus Scriptorum Ecclesiasticorum Latinorum.* Vindobonae: apud C. Geroldi filium, 1866 to date. Vol. 34.

————. *Sermones.* Ed. J. P. Migne. *PL.* Paris: Garnier Fratres, 1844–55. Vol. 38.

Aurelian of Arles. *Regula ad Monachos.* Ed. J. P. Migne. *PL.* Paris: Garnier Fratres, 1874. Vol. 68.

Austin, Gerard, O. P. *Trinitarian Doctrine in the Gallican Liturgy According to the Missale Gothicum.* Paris: Institut Catholique de Paris, 1968.

Axton, Richard. *European Drama of the Early Middle Ages.* London: Hutchinson University Library, 1974.

Bannister, H. M., ed. *A Gallican Sacramentary.* London: Henry Bradshaw Society, 1917. Vols. 52, 54.

Beck, H. G. J. *The Pastoral Care of Souls in South-East France during the Sixth Century.* Romae: apud Aedes Universitatis Gregorianae, 1950.

Beck, Hans Georg. *Kirche und theologische Literatur im Byzantinischen Reich.* Munich: Beck, 1959.

Bede. *De Arte Metrica.* Eds. C. B. Kendall and M. H. King. Typographi Brepols Turnholti, Belgium, 1975. Vol. 123A.

Behrens, Irene. *Die Lehre von der Einteilung der Dichtkunst.* Halle/Saale: Max Niemeyer, 1940.

Bernard d'Angers. *Liber Miraculorum Sancte Fidis.* Ed. A. Bouillet. Paris: Picard, 1897.

Bieber, Margarete. *The History of the Greek and Roman Theater.* 2d ed. Princeton, N.J.: Princeton University Press, 1961.

Bishop, Edmund. "The Genius of the Roman Rite." Rpt. in *Liturgica Historica: Papers on the Liturgy and Religious Life of the Western Church.* Oxford: Clarendon Press, 1918.

Bobbio Missal: A Gallican Mass Book. Ed. E. A. Lowe et al. London: Henry Bradshaw Society, 1917–23. Vols. 53, 58, 61.

Bona, Giovanni (Cardinal). *Rerum Liturgicarum Libri Duo.* Cologne: Hermannus Demen, 1674.

Bonilla y San Martin, Adolfo. *Las Bacantes o del origen de teatro.* Madrid: Rivadeneyra, 1921.

Boor, Helmut de. *Die Textgeschichte der lateinischen Osterfeiern.* Tübingen: Niemayer, 1967.

Bourgeault, Cynthia W. "The Jongleur Art: A Study in Medieval Role-Playing and its Significance for the Cycle Drama." Diss. Univ. of Pennsylvania, 1972.

Bourque, Emmanuel. *Étude sur les sacramentaires romains.* 2 vols. in 3. Rome: Instituto Pontificio di Archeologia Cristiana, 1949; Quebec: Presses Universitaires Laval, 1952 (Vol. II, part I); Rome, 1958 (Vol. II, part 2).

Braulio. *Sancti Braulionis Caesaraugustani Episcopi Vita S. Emiliani.* Edicion Critica por Luis Vazquez de Parga. Madrid: Sucesores de Rivadeneyra, S. A., 1943.

Brault, Gerard J., Ed. *The Song of Roland: An Analytical Edition.* 2 Vols. University Park and London: The Pennsylvania State University Press, 1978.

Brown, Peter. *The Cult of the Saints: Its Rise and Function in Latin Christianity.* Chicago: University of Chicago Press, 1981.

Bruyne, Edgar de. *Études d'esthétique médiévale.* 3 vols. Brugge: De Tempel, 1946.

———. *The Esthetics of the Middle Ages.* Trans. Eileen Hennessy. New York: Frederick Ungar, 1969. (A shortened version of the above item.)

Caesarius of Arles. *Opera Omnia.* Ed. Germain Morin. 2 vols. Maretioli, 1937–42; 2nd ed. *CCSL,* 1953. (The *Vita* of Caesarius appears only in the first edition.)

———. *Sermons.* Trans. Sister Mary Magdeleine Mueller. 3 vols. New York: Fathers of the Church, 1956–73.

Cargill, Oscar. *Drama and Liturgy.* New York: Columbia University Press, 1930.

Carpenter, Marjorie. Trans. *Kontakia of Romanos, Byzantine Melodist.* Columbia: University of Missouri Press, 1970.

Chadwick, Nora. *Poetry and Letters in Early Christian Gaul.* London: Bowes and Bowes, 1955.

Chailley, Jacques. *L'École musicale de Saint-Martial de Limoges jusqu'à la fin du XIᵉ siècle.* Paris: Les Livres Essentiels, 1960.

——. "Un Document nouveau sur la danse ecclésiastique." *Acta Musicologica,* 21 (1949), 18–24.

Chambers, E. K. *The Mediaeval Stage.* 2 vols. Oxford: Oxford University Press, 1903.

Coffman, G. R. *New Theory Concerning the Origin of the Miracle Play.* (Diss. University of Wisconsin, Menasha, Wisconsin: Privately Printed, 1914).

Coless, Gabriel. "Recent Liturgical Study." *American Benedictine Review,* 22 (1971), 387–427.

Collins, Fletcher. *Production of Medieval Church Music Drama.* Charlottesville, Va.: University of Virginia Press, 1972.

Concilia Aevi Karolini. Ed. Albert Werminghoff. Hanoveriae: Impensis Bibliopolii Hahniani, 1904–08. (*MGH,* Legum Section 3.)

Concilia Galliae. A.511–A.695. Ed. Carolus de Clercq. *CCSL.* 1963

Cottas, Vénétia. *Le Théâtre à Byzance.* Paris: Paul Geuthner, 1931.

Craig, Hardin. *English Religious Drama of the Middle Ages.* London: Oxford University Press, 1955.

Curtius, Ernst. *European Literature and the Latin Middle Ages.* Trans. Willard Trask. Princeton, N.J.: Princeton University Press, 1967.

Davidson, Clifford, Ed. *The Saint Play in Medieval Europe.* Kalamazoo, Mich.: Medieval Institute Publications, 1986.

de Labriolle, Pierre. *Histoire de la littérature latine chrétienne.* 3rd ed. 2 vols. Paris: Les Belles-Lettres, 1947.

Delehaye, Hippolyte. *The Legends of the Saints (Les Légendes hagiographiques).* Trans. Donald Attwater. New York: Fordham University Press, 1962.

Deyermond, A. D. *A Literary History of Spain: The Middle Ages.* London: Ernest Benn; New York: Barnes and Noble, 1971.

Dictionary of World Literature. Ed. Joseph Shipley. Rev. ed. New York: Philosophical Library, 1953, Rpt. 1968.

Diomedes. "De Poematibus." *Ars Grammatica,* Book III, in *Grammatici Latini.* Ed. Heinrich Keil. 7 vols. Lipsiae: Teubner, 1855–80, Vol. 1.

Domínguez Bordona, José. *Spanish Illumination.* 1929. New York: Harcourt Brace, 1969.

Donovan, Richard. *The Liturgical Drama in Medieval Spain.* Toronto: Pontifical Institute of Mediaeval Studies, 1958.

Dronke, Peter. "Narrative and Dialogue in Medieval Secular Drama." In *Literature in Fourteenth Century England.* Ed. Piero Boitani and Anna Torti. Tübingen: Gunter Narr; and Cambridge: D. S. Brewer, 1983, pp. 99–120.

Du Cange (Charles Du Fresne). *Glossarium Mediae et Infimae Latinitatis.*

Rev. ed. by Léopold Favre. Paris: Librairie des Sciences et des Arts, 1937.

Duchesne, Louis. *Origines du culte chrétien*. Paris: Ernest Thorin, 1889.

Duckworth, George E. *The Nature of Roman Comedy*. Princeton, N.J.: Princeton University Press, 1952.

Duff, J. Wight. *A Literary History of Rome in the Silver Age*. 2nd ed. London: E. Benn, 1960.

Du Méril, Édélstand. *Les Origines latines du théâtre moderne*. Leipzig, 1897.

Dunn, E. Catherine. "French Medievalists and the Saint's Play: A Problem for American Scholarship." *Medievalia et Humanistica*, New Series 6 (1975), 51–62.

————. "The Origin of the Saints' Plays: The Question Reopened." In *Medieval Drama: A Collection of Festival Papers*. Ed. William A. Selz. Vermillion, S.D.: The Dakota Press, 1968.

————. "The Saint's Legend as History and as Poetry." *American Benedictine Review* 27 (1976), 357–78.

————. "The Saint's Legend as *Mimesis:* Gallican Liturgy and Mediterranean Culture." *Medieval and Renaissance Drama in England*, 1 (1984), 13–27.

————. Review of *Christian Rite and Christian Drama*, by O. B. Hardison. *Catholic Historical Review* 54 (1968–69), 105–6.

Eligius, St. "Vita Eligii Episcopi Noviomagensis" in *MGH: Scriptores Rerum Merovingicarum (Passiones Vitaeque Sanctorum Aevi Merovingicarum)*. Ed. B. Krusch. Hannoverae et Lipsiae: Hahn, 1902. Vol. IV.

Fabre, Augustin, Ed. and trans. *La Chanson de sainte Foy de Conques*. Rodez: Éditions de la Revue historique de Rouergue, 1940.

Fábrega Grau, Ángel, Ed. *Pasionario hispanico*. 2 vols. Madrid–Barcelona: Monumenta Hispaniae Sacra, 1953–55.

Faral, Edmond. *Les Jongleurs en France au Moyen Âge*. Paris: Librairie Honoré Champion, 1910.

Fernández Alonso, Justo. *La Cura pastorale en la Espagña romano-visigoda*. Madrid: Estades, Artes Gráficas, 1955.

Férotin, Dom Marius. *Monumenta Ecclesiae Liturgica*. Paris: Firmin-Didot, 1912. Vol. 6.

Ferreolus. *S. Ferreoli Ucetiensis Episcopi Regula ad Monachos* in Migne, *PL*, 66 (1859), cols. 959–76.

Fétis, F. J. *Histoire générale de la musique*. 5 vols. Paris: F. Didot, 1876.

Flanigan, Clifford. "The Roman Rite and the Origins of the Liturgical Drama." *University of Toronto Quarterly*, 43 (1974), 263–84.

————. "The Fleury *Playbook* and the Traditions of Medieval Latin Drama." *Comparative Drama* 18 (1984–85), 348–72.

————. "The Liturgical Context of the *Quem Quaeritis* Trope." *Comparative Drama* 8 (1974), 45–62.

Fleming, John. *An Introduction to the Franciscan Literature of the Middle Ages.* Chicago: Franciscan Herald Press, 1977.

Foatelli, Renée. *Les Danses religieuses dans la Christianisme.* 2nd ed. Paris: Éditions Spes, 1947.

Fodor's Spain 1975. Ed. Eugene Fodor et al. New York: David McKay, 1975.

Fortini, Arnaldo. *La Lauda in Assisi e le origini del teatro italiano.* A cura della Società internazionale di studi francescani. N.P.: Edizioni Assisi, 1961.

Fortunatus. *Venanti Honori Clementiani Fortunati Opera Poetica.* Ed. Fridericus Leo. *MGH: Auctorum Antiquissimorum,* Vol. 4. Berolini: Apud Weidmannos, 1881.

Frank, Grace. *The Medieval French Drama.* Oxford: Clarendon Press, 1954.

Frugoni, Chiara. "La Rappresentazione dei giullari nelle chiese fino al XII sec." In *Il Contributo dei giullari alla dramaturgia italiana delle origini.* Viterbo: Centro de Studi sul Teatro Mediovale e Rinascimentale, 1977; Rome: Bulzoni, 1978.

Gaiffier, B. de. "La Lecture des Actes des martyrs dans la prière liturgique en Occident." *Analecta Bollandiana* 72 (1954), 134–66.

Gamber, Klaus. *Codices Latini Liturgici Antiquiores.* 2nd ed. Freiburg: Universitätsverlag Freiburg Schweiz, 1968.

———. *Ordo Antiquus Gallicanus: Der gallikanische Messritus des 6 Jh.* Textus Patristici et Liturgici, 3. Regensburg: Verlag Friedrich Pustet, 1965. See Germain, St., de Paris. *Expositio Brevis.*

Gamer, Helena A. "Mimes, Musicians and the Origin of the Medieval Religious Play." *Deutsche Beiträge zur Geistigen Überleiferung,* 5 (1965), 9–28.

García Rodriguez, Carmen. *El Culto de los santos en la España romana y visigoda.* Madrid: C.S.I.C., 1966.

Germain, St., de Paris. Sancti Germani Parisiensis Episcopi. *Expositio Brevis Antiquae Liturgiae Gallicanae in Duas Epistolas Digesta.* Ed. J. P. Migne. *PL,* Vol. 72 (1878). (See also Klaus Gamber.)

Gougaud, L. "La Danse dans les églises." *Revue d'histoire ecclésiastique,* 15 (1914), 5–22.

Gregory of Tours. *The History of the Franks.* Trans. O. M. Dalton. 2 vols. Oxford: Clarendon Press, 1927. Rpt. 1967.

———. *Libri Historiarum X.* Ed. Bruno Krusch and Wilhelm Levison, 2nd ed. Hannoverae: Impensis Bibliopoli Hahniani, 1951.

———. *Miracula et Opera Minora.* Ed. Bruno Krusch, *MGH.* Hanover: Hahn, 1885, Rpt. 1969.

Griffe, É. "Aux Origines de la liturgie gallicane." *Bulletin de littérature ecclésiastique de Toulouse,* 52 (1951), 17–43.

———. *La Gaule chrétienne à l'époque romain,* 3 vols. Paris: Picard, 1947; Letouzey and Ané, 1964.

Grosdidier de Matons, J. *Romanos le Mélode et les origines de la poésie religieuse à Byzance.* Paris: Beauchesne, 1977.

Guerrero Lovillo, José. *Las Cántigas: Estudio arqueólogico de sus miniaturas.* Madrid: Consejo Superior de Investigaciones Científicas. Instituto Diego Velázquez, 1949.

Hardison, O. B. *Christian Rite and Christian Drama in the Middle Ages.* Baltimore: Johns Hopkins Press, 1965.

Hillgarth, J. N. "Popular Religion in Visigothic Spain." In *Visigothic Spain: New Approaches.* Ed. Edward James. Oxford: Clarendon Press, 1980.

Holmes, Urban Tigner. *History of Old French Literature from the Origins to 1300.* Rev. ed. New York: Russell and Russell, 1962.

Hone, William. *Ancient Mysteries Described.* London: Printed for William Hone, 1823, Rpt. Singing Tree Press, Book Tower, 1969.

Huizinga, J. *Homo Ludens.* New York: Roy Publishers, 1950.

Hult, David F. "The Limits of Mimesis: Notes Toward a Generic Revision of Medieval Theater." *L' Esprit Créateur,* 23 (1983), 49–63.

Hunningher, Benjamin. *The Origin of the Theater.* The Hague, 1955; New York: Hill and Wang, 1961.

Hurtado y J. de la Serna, Juan, and Ángel González-Palencia. *Historia de la literatura española.* Madrid: SAETA, 1949.

Ildefonso de Toldeo, San. *La Virginitad perpetua de Santa Maria.* Ed. and trans. Vicente Blanco Garcia. Santos Padres Españoles, Vol. 1. Madrid: Biblioteca de Autores Cristianos, 1971.

Isidore of Seville. *Etymologiae.* Ed. W. M. Lindsay. 2 vols. Oxford: Clarendon Press, 1911.

Jauss, Hans-Robert. *Toward an Aesthetic of Reception.* Trans. Timothy Bahti. Minneapolis: University of Minnesota Press, 1982. (Vol. 2 of the series *Theory and History of Literature.*)

Jeffrey, David. "Franciscan Spirituality and the Rise of Early English Drama." *Mosaic 8* (1974–75), 17–46.

Jones, Leslie W., and C. R. Morey. *The Miniatures of the Manuscripts of Terence Prior to the Thirteenth Century.* 2 vols. Princeton, N.J.: Princeton University Press, 1930–31.

Jungmann, Joseph. *The Mass of the Roman Rite.* Trans. F. A. Brunner. New York: Benziger, 1951, 1959.

King, Archdale A. *Liturgies of the Past.* London: Longmans Green, 1959; Milwaukee: Bruce Publishing, 1959.

———. *The Rites of Eastern Christendom.* 2 vols. New York: AMS Reprint, 1972 of the 1947 edition, Rome: Tipografia Poliglotta Vaticana, 1947.

Klauser, Theodor. *A Short History of the Western Liturgy.* Trans. John Halliburton. London: Oxford University Press, 1969.

Knowles, David. *Great Historical Enterprises.* London: Thomas Nelson, 1963.

Kristeller, Paul. "Humanism and Scholasticism in the Italian Renaissance." *Byzantion*, 17 (1944–45), 346–74.

La Drière, J. Craig. "Voice and Address." *Dictionary of World Literature: Criticism—Forms—Techniques*. Ed. Joseph Shipley. Rev. ed. New York: Philosophical Library, 1953, Rpt. 1968.

Laistner, Max. *Thought and Letters in Western Europe, A.D. 500–900*. Rev. ed., Ithaca, N.Y.: Cornell University Press, 1957.

La Piana, George. *Le Rappresentazioni sacre nella letteratura bizantina*. Grottaferrata: S. Nilo, 1912.

———. "The Byzantine Theatre." *Speculum*, 11 (1936), 171–211.

Leclercq, Henri. "Gallicane (Liturgie)." *Dictionnaire d'archéologie chrétienne et de liturgie*. Paris: Letouzey and Ané, 1924, Vol. VI.

———. *Mabillon*. 2 vols. Paris: Letouzey and Ané, 1953–57.

Leclercq, Jean. "Joculator et Saltator: S. Bernard et l'image du jongleur dans les manuscrits." In *Translatio Studii: Honoring O. L. Kapsner*. Collegeville, Minn.: St. John's University Press, 1973, pp. 124–48.

———. "Le Thème de la jonglerie chez St. Bernard et ses contemporains." *Revue d'histoire de la spiritualité*, 48 (1972), 385–400.

Liber Commicus. Ed. Germain Morin. Maredsous: Desclée, De Brouwer, 1893.

———. Ed. Fray Justo Perez de Urbel and Atilano González y Ruiz-Zorrilla. 2 vols. Madrid: C. Bermejo, 1950–55.

Lienhard, Joseph J. *Paulinus of Nola and Early Western Monasticism*. Cologne: P. Hanstein, 1977.

Lindsay, Jack. *Byzantium into Europe*. London: Bodley Head, 1952.

Lipphardt, Walter. *Lateinische Osterfeiern und Osterspiele*. 7 vols. Berlin and New York: De Gruyter, 1975–83.

Lipsius, Richard Adelbert, Ed. *Acta Apostolorum Apocrypha post Constantinum Tischendorf*, denuo ediderunt Ricardus Adelbertus Lipsius et Maximilianus Bonnet. Lipsiae: Apud Hermannum Mendelssohn, 1891–98.

Lowrie, Walter. *Art in the Early Church*. New York: Harper and Row, 1965.

Mabillon, Jean. *De Liturgia Gallicana Libri Tres*. Ed. J. P. Migne. *PL*, Vol. 72.

———. *De Cursu Gallicano Disquisitio*. Ed. J. P. Migne, *PL*, Vol. 72.

McGuire, Martin R. *Introduction to Medieval Latin Studies*. 2nd ed. Washington, D.C.: The Catholic University of America Press, 1977.

Mâle, É. *La Fin du paganisme en Gaule*. Paris: Flammarion, 1950.

Malnory, A. *Saint Césaire, Évêque d'Arles, 503–43*. Paris: Librairie Émile Bouillon, 1894. Rpt. Slatkine, 1978.

Mansi, J. D., Ed. *Sacrorum Conciliorum et Decretorum Nova et Amplissima Collectio*. Leipzig: Welter, 1901.

Marignan, A. *Le Culte des saints sous les Mérovingiens*. (*Études sur la civilization française*, Vol. II.) Paris: Émile Bouillon, 1899.

Marshall, Mary. "'Theatre' in the Middle Ages: Evidence from Dictionaries and Glosses." *Symposium*, 4 (1950), 1–39.

Martène, Edmond. *De Antiquis Ecclesiae Ritibus Libri Quattuor*. Rotomagi: G. Behourt, 1700.

————. *Tractatus de Antiqua Ecclesiae Disciplina in Divinis Celebrandis Officiis*. 4 vols. Lugdini, 1706.

Menéndez Pidal, Ramón. *Poesía juglaresca y origines de las literaturas romanicas*. 6th ed. Madrid: Instituto de Estudios Politicos, 1957.

————. *Poesía juglaresca y juglares*. 6th ed. Madrid: Espasa-Calpe, S. A., 1969. (A paperback and shortened edition of the above item.)

Miller, James L. *Measures of Wisdom*. Toronto: University of Toronto Press, 1986.

Missale Gallicanum Vetus. Ed. L. Cunibert Mohlberg, P. Siffrin, and L. Eisenhöfer. *Rerum Ecclesiasticarum Documenta*, Rome: Herder, 1958.

Missale Gothicum. Ed. L. Cunibert Mohlberg. Augsburg: Benno Filser Verlag, 1929.

Mone, F. J. *Messen Lateinische und Greichische*. Frankfurt, 1850.

Moraleda y Esteban, Juan. *Los Seises de la Catedral de Toledo: Antiqüedad, Vestidos, Música y Danza*. Toledo: A. Garijo, 1911.

Morin, Germain. "The Homilies of St. Caesarius of Arles." *Orate Fratres*, 14 (1939–40), 481–86.

Muller, H. F. "Pre-History of the Medieval Drama: the Antecedents of the Tropes and the Conditions of Their Appearance." *Zeitschrift für Romanische Philologie*, 44 (1924), 544–75.

Muratori, Lodovico. *Antiquitates Italicae Medii Aevi*. 17 vols. Mediolani, Italy: Societas Palatina, 1739. Vol. 2.

Neale, John, and G. H. Forbes. *The Ancient Liturgies of the Gallican Church*. 1855–67. New York: AMS Press, 1970.

Netzer, H. (Abbé). *L'Introduction de la Messe romaine en France sous les Carolingiens*. Avec préface par A. Clerval. Paris: A. Picart, 1910; Farnborough: Gregg, 1968.

Neunheuser, Burkhard. "Die Römische Liturgie in ihren Beziehungen zur Fränkisch-Germanischen Kultur und der Tropus." In *Dimensioni Drammatiche della Liturgia Medioevale: Atti del I Convegno di Studio Viterbo*. Viterbo: Bulzoni Editore, 1977, pp. 161–68.

Nicoll, Allardyce. *Masks, Mimes and Miracles: Studies in the Popular Theatre*. New York: Cooper Square, 1963.

Norwood, Gilbert. *The Art of Terence*. 1923. New York: Russell and Russell, 1965.

Ogilvy, J. D. A. "*Mimi, Scurrae, Histriones*: Entertainers of the Early Middle Ages." *Speculum*, 38 (1963) 603–19.

Olsen, Glending. *Literature as Recreation in the Middle Ages*. Ithaca, N.Y.: Cornell University Press, 1982.

Oxford Book of Carols. London: Oxford University Press, 1928, 1964.

Oxford Latin Dictionary. Oxford: Clarendon Press, 1977.

Passiones Vitaeque Sanctorum Aevi Merovingici et Antiquiorum Aliquot. Ed. Bruno Krusch. Hanoverae: Impensis Bibliopolii Hahniani, 1896. (*MGH, Scriptores Rerum Merovingicarum*, Vols. III–VII.)

Paulinus of Nola. *Carmina.* Ed. Guilelmus De Hartel. *CSEL*, Vol. 30. Vienna, 1894; *Epistulae, CSEL*, Vol. 29.

————. *The Poems of St. Paulinus of Nola.* Trans. and annotated P. G. Walsh. New York: Newman Press, 1975.

Porter, William S. *The Gallican Rite.* London: Mowbray, 1958.

Quasten, Johannes. "Gallican Rites." *New Catholic Encyclopedia.* New York: Harcourt Brace, 1967. Vol. VI.

————. *Music and Worship in Pagan and Christian Antiquity.* Trans. Boniface Ramsey. Washington, D.C.: National Association of Pastoral Musicians, 1983.

————. *Musik und Gesang in den Kulten der heidnischen Antike und Christlichen Frühzeit.* Münster: Aschendorff, 1930, 1973.

————. "Oriental Influence in the Gallican Liturgy." *Traditio* 1 (1943), 55–78.

Raby, F. J. *A History of Christian-Latin Poetry.* 2d ed. Oxford: Clarendon Press, 1953.

Rahner, Karl. *The Christian Commitment: Essays in Pastoral Theology.* Trans. Cecily Hastings. New York: Sheed and Ward, 1963.

Raynouard, M. *Choix des poésies originales des troubadours,* 1816–21; Rpt. Osnabrück: Biblio-Verlag, 1966, Vol. 2.

Reich, Hermann. *Der Mimus: Ein litterar-entwickelungsgeschichtlicher Versuch.* Berlin: Weidmann, 1903; New York: G. Olms, 1974.

Rey-Flaud, Henri. *Le Cercle magique: Essai sur le théâtre en rond à la fin du moyen-âge.* Paris: Gallimard, 1973.

Riché, Pierre. *Éducation et Culture dans l'Occident barbare, VIe–VIIIe siècles.* Paris: Éditions de Seuil, 1962.

————. *Education and Culture in the Barbarian West, 6th–8th Centuries.* Trans. John Contreni. Columbia, S.C.: University of South Carolina Press, 1976.

Rosa y López, de la, Simón. *Los Seises de la Catedral de Sevilla.* Sevilla: Imp. de Francisco de P. Díaz, 1904.

Roy, Bruno. "Arnulf of Orléans and the Latin Comedy." *Speculum* 49 (1974), 258–66.

Salmon, Pierre. Ed. *Le Lectionnaire de Luxeuil. Collectanea Biblica Latina* 7 (1944) and 9 (1953).

Salvian. *De Gubernatione Dei.* Ed. Carolus Halm. *MGH.* Berlin: Weidmann, 1877.

————. *The Writings of Salvian, the Presbyter.* Trans. Jeremiah O'Sullivan. Washington, D.C.: The Catholic University of America Press, 1962.

Schnusenberg, Christine. *Das Verhältnis von Kirche und Theater.* Bern: Peter Lang, 1981.

Sepet, Marius. *Origines catholiques du théâtre moderne.* Paris: Lethielleux, 1904.

Servius, *Commentarii.* Ed. Thilo and Hagen. Lipsiae: Teubner, 1887.

Shergold, N. D. *A History of the Spanish Stage from Medieval Times until the End of the Seventeenth Century.* Oxford: Clarendon Press, 1967.

Sidonius Apollinaris. *Epistulae et Carmina.* Ed. Christianus Loetjohann. *MGH*, Auct. Ant. Berlin, 1887, Vol. 8.

———. Ed. P. Mohr. Leipzig: Teubner, 1895.

———. *The Letters of Sidonius.* Trans. O. M. Dalton. 2 vols. Oxford: Clarendon Press, 1915.

Souter, Alexander. *A Glossary of Later Latin to 600 A.D.* Oxford: Clarendon Press, 1949.

Stevens, C. E. *Sidonius Apollinaris and His Age.* Oxford: Clarendon Press, 1933.

Sticca, Sandro. "The *Christos Paschon* and the Byzantine Theater." *Comparative Drama* 8 (1974), 13–44.

———. *The Latin Passion Play: Its Origins and Development.* Albany: State University of New York Press, 1970.

Sulpicius Severus. *Sulpicii Severi Opera.* Ed. C. Halm. *CSEL.*, 1966. Vol. 1.

Taladoire, Barthélemy A. *Commentaires sur la mimique et l'expression corporelle du comédien romain.* Montpellier, France: Déhan, 1951.

Thibaut, Jean-Baptiste. *L'Ancienne liturgie gallicane.* Paris: Maison de la Bonne Presse, 1929.

Thompson, E. A. *The Goths in Spain.* Oxford: Clarendon Press, 1969.

Tillyard, H. J. W. *Byzantine Music and Hymnography.* London: The Faith Press, 1923 (AMS reprint, 1976).

Trypanes, Konstantinos A. *Medieval and Modern Greek Poetry.* Oxford: Clarendon Press, 1951.

———. Ed. *Sancti Romani Melodi Cantica Genuina.* Oxford: Clarendon Press, 1963.

Uitti, Karl D. *Story, Myth and Celebration in Old French Narrative Poetry, 1050–1200.* Princeton, N.J.: Princeton University Press, 1973.

Van Dam, Raymond. *Leadership and Community in Late Antique Gaul.* Berkeley and Los Angeles: University of California Press, 1985.

Varro, M. Terenti Varronis. *De Lingua Latina quae Supersunt.* Ed. Georgius Goetz and Fridericus Schoell. Lipsiae: Teubner, 1910.

Velimirovic, Milos M. "Liturgical Drama in Byzantium and Russia." *Dumbarton Oaks Papers* 16 (1962), 351–85.

Villoslada, Ricardo García, Ed. *Historia de la iglesia en España.* Madrid: Biblioteca de Autores Cristianos, 1979, Vol. I: "La Iglesia en la España romana y visigoda."

Visigothic Spain: New Approaches. Ed. Edward James. Oxford: Clarendon Press, and New York: Oxford University Press, 1980.

Vives, José. *Concilios Visigóticos e Hispano-Romanos,* Ed. José Vives. Barcelona–Madrid: Consejo Superior de Investigaciones Científicas, 1963.

Vogel, Cyrille. "Le Développement historique du culte chrétien en occident." *Problemi di storia della Chiesa: l'Alto Medioevo.* Milano: Vita e Pensiero, 1973, II, 73–97.

———. *Introduction aux sources de l'histoire du culte chrétien au moyen âge.* Spoleto: Centro Italiano di Studi sull'Alto Medioevo, n.d.

Wall, Catherine Louise. *A Study of "The Appearance of Our Lady to St. Thomas": Pageant XLVI in the York Cycle of Mystery Plays.* Ann Arbor, Mich.: University Microfilms, 1965.

Wardropper, Bruce W. *Historia de la poesía lirica a lo divino en la cristiandad occidental.* Madrid: Revista de Occidente, 1958.

Warning, Rainer. "On the Alterity of Medieval Religious Drama." *New Literary History* 10 (1979), 265–92.

Wellesz, Egon. *A History of Byzantine Music and Hymnography.* 2nd ed. Oxford: Clarendon Press, 1961.

Wickham, Glynne. *The Medieval Theatre.* 3rd ed. Cambridge: Cambridge University Press, 1987.

Woolf, Rosemary. *The English Mystery Plays.* Berkeley and Los Angeles: University of California Press, 1972.

Wulfstan. *The Miracles of St. Wulfstan.* Ed. Reginald Darlington. London: The Royal Society, 1928.

Young, Karl. *The Drama of the Medieval Church.* 2 vols. Oxford: Clarendon Press, 1933.

Zimmerman, Ernst Heinrich. *Die Vorkarolingischen Miniaturen.* 5 vols. Berlin: Selbstverlag des Deutschen Vereins für Kunstwissenschaft, 1916.

Zumthor, Paul. "The Text and the Voice." *New Literary History* 16 (1984), 67–92. (Trans. Marilyn Engelhardt.)

INDEX

The Gallican and Hispanic liturgical texts, with their editors, are discussed in chronological order in the bibliographical chapter (II), and have not been indexed here.

Agobard of Lyons, 32
Alessandro, Silvio, 105
Alfaric, Prosper and Ernest Hoepffner, 58, 110, 113, 143
Ambrosian rite, 27
Andrieu, Michel, 20
Anglès, Higini, 106
Aquitaine, 63
Arian heresy, 11, 56
Arles, 29, 30, 87, 88
Aubé, Benjamin, 57–58
Augustine, St., and the principle of the *contrafactum*, 7, 143; homilies, 141; miracles of St. Stephen, recorded, 89, 95–97; opposition to festival dancing, 58–59
Aurelian of Arles, 87
Austin, Gerard, 36

Baile, popular dance entertainment, Spanish, 116–117
Bieber, Margarete, 52–55
Bishop, Edmund, 19
Bona, Cardinal Joannes, 23
Bonilla y San Martin, Adolfo, 104, 144
Bourque, Emmanuel, 20
Braulio, Bishop, life of St. Aemilian, 98–100
Brown, Peter, 7, 8, 33, 79
Bruyne, Edgar de, 50–51

Caesarius, bishop of Arles, 1, 24–25, 27, 29, 30, 64, 67, 71, 101, 110, 112, 119, 121, 122, 140–43
Calliopius, 4
Cargill, Oscar, 14
Carpenter, Marjorie, 13
Castile, drama of, 103–6
Chadwick, Nora, 63, 67
Chailley, Jacques, 118, 120
Chambers, E. K., 71–72, 118–19, 124, 125, 129, 136, 137, 139
Charles the Bald, 25
Choreia, 109
Coffman, G. R., 87
Contestatio, Gallican, 79–83
Contrafactum, 55–59, 71, 106, 113
Cottas, Vénétia, 8, 11, 60–62, 109
Councils, Church: Agde, 30; Auxerre, 108–9; Avignon, 109–10; Braga, 31; Carthage III, 30; Chalon, 109; Laodicea, 31; Toledo III, 30, 69, 107–8; Tours, 30; and liturgical dance, 107–10; and saints' festival liturgy, 30–32
Craig, Hardin, 143–44
Curtius, Ernst, 49–50

Dance, at the pervigilium, 57; Conciliar condemnations, 107–11; Hispanic tradition, 104–6; of *seises*, 115; popular, 116–17; sacred, 57–59; St. John Baptist's day, 111–12; St. Martial's feast, 117–19; St. William of Orange's feast, 119; Sens Cathedral,

120–21; Seville, 114–15; Toledo, 113–14
Davidson, Clifford, 146
Deconstructionist theory, 7, 47, 49
Donovan, Richard, 37, 103–5
Drama, nature of ancient Greek and Byzantine, 11, 12; Byzantine, 9–13, 55–62; continuity of ancient, 3–4, 46–53, 143–44; Roman, 47–55, 129
Drama *vs.* liturgy, 59
Du Méril, Édélstand, 122, 123

Fábrega Grau, Ángel, 97
Fabula, as conversation, 27–28, 51; as drama, 51–52
Faral, Edmond, 13, 125, 132, 139
Feier (ritual) *vs. Speil* (play), 59
Fernández Alonso, Justo, 108
Ferreolus of Uzès, 87–88
Fétis, François, 19
Flanigan, Clifford, 6–7, 21, 38, 47–49, 146
Foatelli, Renée, 111–113, 119
Francis of Assisi, and *juglaría*, 138
Frank, Grace, 3–4, 6, 9, 15, 47–48
Frugoni, Chiara, 137–38

Gaiffier, B. de, 64, 79
Gallican liturgical texts, modern editions of, 35–42
Gallican liturgy, suppression of, 144–45
Gallican *vs.* Gallic liturgies, 36
Germain d'Auxerre, St., 81–82
Germain de Paris, pseudo-, 21, 26–28
Gougaud, L., 102, 117
Grammarians, late Latin and dramatic tradition, 48–53: Bede, 51; Diomedes, 49–51; Donatus, 48; Isidore of Seville, 51; Servius, 48
Gregory of Tours, 1, 21, 25, 41–42, 73–74, 86–87
Griffe, É., 18, 39, 79

Hardison, O. B., 1, 20, 136
Hilduin, Abbot of St. Denys, 25

Hill Monastic Library, 40, 90
Hispanic (Mozarabic) liturgical texts, editions of, 42–45
Huizinga, J., 59
Hunningher, Benjamin, 14, 55

Inlatio (illatio), Hispanic, 82–83

Jauss, Hans-Robert, 6, 48–49
Joculatores, See *Juglaría*
Jongleurs, See *Juglaría*
Juglaría (jonglerie, minstrelsy), ancient attitudes toward, 127–29; as international phenomenon, 122–26; favorable medieval recognition, 133–36; generic sense, 101, 123; medieval attitudes, 130–31; participation in church life, 136–38; relation to ancient Latin entertainment, 124

King, Archdale, 56
Konstanz, school of, 47
Kontakion, 10, 61

LaDrière, J. Craig, 49
La Piana, George, 8, 10, 13, 60–62
Leclercq, Henri, 19, 22–23
Leclercq, Jean, *juglaría* and ecclesiastical attitudes, 136–38
Lections, Byzantine, 9; Gallican, 18, 23–26, 31, 40, 89, 95, 142; Hispanic, 94–100; *legendarium*, 88–89; *passionarium*, 88
Liber commicus, Spanish, 43–44, 95
Lipphardt, Walter, 59
Liturgy, Byzantine, 8–13, 55–58, 60–62; Gallic, 25, 36; Gallican, 17–18, 22–27, 35, 73; Hispanic (Mozarabic), 25, 27, 36, 42–43; Roman, 1, 31–32
Roman *vs.* Gallican features, 19–22
López, de la Rosa y, Simón, 114–15
Louis the Pious, 25
Luxeuil Lectionary, 8, 89–94

Mabillon, Jean, 17, 73, 77, 80, 98; *De Cursu Gallicano*, 28–32, 87–88; *De Liturgia Gallicana*, 23–27; discovery of the Luxeuil Lectionary, 18; viewpoints compared with modern, 33–34

Marignan, A., 18, 75–77, 86
Marshall, Mary, 4
Martène, Edmond, 26, 31
Matins office, 29, 83–85, 88, 103, 105, 108
Menéndez Pidal, Ramón, on favorable attitudes toward *juglaría*, 133–36; on Gonzalo de Berceo, 138; on narrative *juglares vs.* lyrical, 131; on negative attitudes to *juglaría*, 127; on the origins and nature of *juglaría*, 123–26
Mime, Byzantine, 9
Mime, history of, 5–6, 10, 11–13, 59, 60–61, 65–71, 102, 110, 116, 124, 129–30, 140, 145
Mimi, 72, 85, 126, 128, 131
Minstrelsy. See *juglaría*.
Mone Masses, 37, 82
Moraleda y Esteban, Juan, 103, 105, 106, 114, 115
Morin, Germain, ed., Caesarius of Arles, *Opera Omnia*, 69–71, 142–43
Mozarabic liturgy, definition of, 36–37; See also Hispanic liturgical texts
Mueller, Sister M. Magdeleine, trans. *Sermons*, Caesarius of Arles, 69, 142–43
Muller, H. F., 31, 32, 74

Netzer, H., 28
Neunheuser, Burkhard, 21
Nicoll, Allardyce, 129

Pantomime, 11, 53–54
Paulinus of Nola, 78–79
Perez de Urbel, Justo, 90
Polyeuctus, St., 57–58
Porter, W. S., 101
Provence, and Classical humanism, 63–71, 112; records of, 1

Quasten, Johannes, "Gallican Rites," 18, 23, 38, 60; *Music and Worship*, trans. Boniface Ramsey, 56–59; "Oriental Influence in the Gallican Liturgy," 24; principle of the *contrafactum*, 56–59

Reich, Hermann, 66
Rezeptionsästhetik, 7, 47–9
Romanos, the Melodist, of Byzantiuim, 10, 56

Sacramentary, meaning of, 38
Saints' lives, as center of Gallican culture, 32–34, 76–77
Saints' lives in Gallican liturgy; in the *contestatio*, 80; St. Germain d'Auxerre, 81; St. Remigius, 80
Saints' lives, in Hispanic liturgy, in the *inlatio*, St. Clement, 82; St. Martin, 83; in the *liber commicus*, St. Aemilian (San Millán de la Cogolla), 26, 98–100; Assumption of Mary, 97–98; St. Helena, 89; St. Martin, 83; St. Stephen, 95–97
Saints lives, in lections of Matins and Mass, 85–88; St. Andrew, 41; St. Felix, 78–79; St. Julian, 41; Sts. Julian and Basilissa, 90–91; St. Martial, 117–19; St. Martin, 41; Sts. Peter and Paul, 92–93; St. Polycarp, 25
Salmon, Pierre, 8, 18, 20, 23, 25, 26, 35, 40, 77; Gallican political life, 76; Reading of saints' lives in Gaul, 84–85; the Luxeuil lectionary, 88, 90–94
Salvian, *De Gubernatione Dei*, 65–66
Schnusenberg, Christine, 130
Seises, Spanish, as boy choristers and dancers, 114–15
Sepet, Marius, and continuity of ancient and medieval drama, 12
Sidonius Apollinaris, 66–67
Silence, in Gallican liturgy, 27–28
Silos, monastery of, 90, 91
Souter, Alexander, 110
Sticca, Sandro, 13

Taladoire, Barthélemy, 5–7
Terence, 15; and Calliopius as editor, 4
Toledo, *seises* as boy choristers and dancers, 113; use of Hispanic rite into the Carolingian era, 35; See also Councils, Toledo III
Tragados, 12
Troparion, 10

Van Dam, Raymond, 33, 76
Visigothic invasions, and Gallican liturgy, 1, 63, 76; and Hispanic liturgy, 107–8
Vogel, Cyrille, 20–21, 42, 145

Wardropper, Bruce, the principle of the *contrafactum* (*a lo divino*), 55–56

Wellesz, Egon, 8, 10, 11, 61, 62
Woolf, Rosemary, 14–15

Young, Karl, 2–4, 6, 7, 15, 47, 54, 91–92, 144–45; rejection of continuity in ancient and medieval drama, 2–4; rejection of continuity in Byzantine and Western medieval drama, 8, 15